# For His Sake

By
Mildred Schrock

Cover Art: David W. Miller

Christian Light Publications, Inc.
Harrisonburg, Virginia 22801

ISBN 0-87813-506-5

Printed in U.S.A.

**Dedicated to**

the memory of my Mother,
whose remarkable memory
made it possible for me to write
this account.

**Acknowledgments**

My thanks to my family and friends who encouraged and assisted me in various ways; and a special note of thanks to Marlene Kropf, great granddaughter of the Joseph Schrags, who so graciously took time to check and type my manuscript in readiness for the press.

—Mildred Schrock

iii

## Foreword

The heroine of this book, Barbara Graber Schrag, and her family, were among the group of Mennonites emigrating to America from Russia in 1874. The story begins in Germany, where these peace-loving people settled following their flight from one country to another seeking freedom from compulsory military service. Their journeys over the years had taken them from Switzerland—where the earliest record of the Graber family name was found—to France, Austria, Poland and Germany. Finally, they migrated to Russia in acceptance of an invitation extended by Queen Catherine II, who promised them absolute freedom for one hundred years. When conditions changed after a period of years and the guarantee was withdrawn, plans were again made for emigration, this time to America.

Barbara and Joseph Schrag were the author's grandparents, and their daughter Fannie, the author's mother. All of the events recorded are true, and the names of the main characters portrayed are the actual names (with the exception of Mr. Jenkins, Drs. Meade, Barnes, Whittier, and Barrows). It was customary then to give a child the name of a previously deceased brother or sister.

The material for this book was supplied by my mother, who had heard her own mother relate their experiences many times. Mother was endowed with an unusually good memory and was a gifted storyteller; thus my childhood was well punctuated with vivid accounts of these true happenings. The one that impressed me most as a child was that of the "Little Red Apron." Though the apron itself never crossed the waters to America, its history did. This along with other unusual happenings prompted me to write this book.

I trust my efforts will, in a measure, help to acquaint the descendants with the history and experiences of their ancestors, and to inspire in them a greater appreciation for the Christian heritage that is theirs. I trust also that readers beyond the family group may find in this account an urgent appeal to follow Christ's way of peace and love.

# PART 1

# CHAPTER

# 1

It was a sunny day in early June. The warm sun shone on a little stone cottage over which red roses climbed and bloomed in profusion. Their fragrance was wafted into the house by an afternoon breeze which gently stirred the snow-white curtains at the open window. Barbara Strauss took the last round, crusty loaf of bread from the oven of the large brick stove and placed it to cool beside the other loaves on the small well-scrubbed table standing nearby. She wiped a bit of perspiration from her damp forehead with the corner of her homespun apron. My, it was warm! But now that her baking was finished the big stove would soon cease to give out so much heat. Like any good housewife, Frau Strauss experienced a feeling of satisfaction at the sight of the freshly baked bread; and the delicious aroma which filled the room and drifted out the open door made her feel amply rewarded for her efforts.

Baby Elizabeth, a golden-haired, winsome little lass of fifteen months, was taking her afternoon nap. Peter, seven, and Joseph, nearly nine, were in school at Weirhof, the little German village about a mile away. School would keep only a few more days, and like any schoolboys, the two lads were eagerly looking forward to the time when lessons would be done. Annie was four, and what a bright-eyed, inquisitive little body she was! She was always running about hither and yon, picking flowers chasing butterflies, or asking endless questions. She was out now with her father in the garden trying to help in her own eager way.

The house was so quiet. Barbara longed to rest awhile or to go out among the flowers she loved so well, but she quickly brushed aside the thought. She glanced first at the spinning wheel in the corner, then at her knitting on her chair. She would get at her knitting, she told herself, and moved her chair closer to the open door. She was knitting a pair of stockings for Joseph, her eldest son. The lad was so hard on them. True, they were not needed now, for the children were going barefoot these warm days, but the summer months had a way of passing swiftly by, and the chilly weather would be upon them all too soon. The winters in Germany were extremely cold, and warm clothing was needed. It was Barbara's task to provide all the clothing for her growing family, so there were not many idle moments for her.

As her fingers flew busily and the bright needles flashed steadily back and forth, Barbara's thoughts were busy too. "At least I can think and work too," she told herself with a little smile. She found her thoughts going back—back over a long period of years, back to the time when life was not so sweet and pleasant as now. Indeed Barbara Strauss and her husband Johann could recall the time when they had undergone severe hardships, for they were numbered among the early Anabaptists, later called Mennonites, who because of their strong belief in the Bible teaching of nonresistance and their undying faith in God, had been forced to flee from one country to another in search of religious freedom.

Barbara's mother had often told her how in the year 1790, twelve years before Barbara was born, they, together with the Krehbiels, Mullers, Strausses, and other families, had left their homes in France and sought refuge in Austria. Only seven short years elapsed until they were forced to flee again, emigrating this time to Poland. Here Barbara was born and here she spent her early childhood days. She remembered vividly the time when she was thirteen that they were compelled once more for the sake of conscience to leave their homes and all that was near and dear to them, arriving at last in Germany and settling near Edwardsdorf.

Barbara paused for a moment, and her knitting dropped unnoticed into her lap. Her eyes rested on the blooming geranium on the windowsill. It was such a bright spot in her kitchen! A bright spot too in her life, she recalled, was

7

the day she and young Johann Strauss exchanged their marriage vows, just four years following their flight into Germany. Johann was a noble, stalwart young man. His deep bass voice rang out above the others in church on Sundays and thrilled the hearts of the listeners. And he was always so gentle and kind. Life looked bright and rosy to the young couple as they began it together in their own little home. Surely their wanderings were over, for the country was peaceable, and they loved this land with its magnificent forests, rolling hills, and fertile plains.

When, a year later, little Joseph was born, their cup of happiness was full.

Barbara resumed her knitting with renewed vigor. She was getting back to the present. God had been good to them, the years had gone rapidly by, and now by hard work and frugal living they were able to call the little farm their own. Johann raised vegetables, and on market day they went to Edwardsdorf to sell their produce. Sometimes Barbara made cheese and butter, and there were eggs occasionally from her little flock of hens. For this extra produce she found a ready sale, and the city folks were glad to purchase the fresh farm products from this cheerful, neat-appearing housewife.

Suddenly baby Elizabeth's cry broke rudely into Barbara's long reverie, and laying her knitting aside, she went into the adjoining room to get her.

"Did you have a good nap, Precious?" The mother greeted her little one tenderly. The

8

baby had been named Maria Elizabeth, but they had ended up calling her Elizabeth. Little Elizabeth smiled happily, and every trace of tears vanished as she stretched out her plump little arms to her mother. Barbara picked her up and held her close.

Annie came running in and called, "Mother, Marie is coming and now I can play with Lena." She clapped her hands delightedly. There was no other little girl whom Annie would rather play with than Lena Kauffman, a little girl about her own age.

Peter Kauffmans lived down the road a short distance. They were the Strauss' closest neighbors, and the two families spent many happy times together. The children enjoyed each other's company, and the two young mothers found much in common while Peter Kauffman and Johann Strauss had always been close friends.

Barbara greeted Marie affectionately in true German fashion. "Come in, Marie dear, and rest yourself." She bustled about and drew up a chair for her friend.

"Good day, Barbara. No, thank you, I must not sit down." She hesitated; her sweet face wore a sad expression, and her eyes looked strangely bright and worried. "I can't stay long today. Henry and Katie will be coming home from school soon, you know," she added with a glance at the big clock on the wall. "I just had to tell you what Peter heard at the village today. Such sad news!" Marie's voice trembled.

Barbara's face paled and a strange fear

gripped her heart. "Marie, what has happened to bring you such sorrow? Tell me quickly."

"Well, Peter heard some officials talking. They were from Edwardsdorf, I believe, and they said our country is—"

"Not at war?" Barbara broke in excitedly.

"Yes, and they are going to call every able-bodied man to arms. Oh, what shall we do? For of course they will take our husbands." She spoke brokenly, tears coming into her eyes.

Barbara put her arms around her friend, and the two young women clung to each other. "We can pray. God will take care of us, and no matter what may come, they cannot take our faith in God," said Barbara bravely, her own heart being cheered a little at the comforting thought.

"Ach, yes, I know, but, oh, will we have to leave our homes again? How can we bear it?" Marie's voice was pathetic.

They talked a little longer; then calling to Lena who was playing with Annie and her little sister, Marie said, "Come, Lena, we must hurry home. I expect Henry and Katie are there already."

Bidding each other a tender goodby, Frau Kauffman and her little daughter hastened home.

Barbara could scarcely contain herself until Marie and Lena were out of her sight. Rushing out to the far end of the garden where Johann was hoeing around the young corn, she told him of Marie's visit and the dreadful news.

Johann dropped his hoe. His own heart grew

heavy as his wife told him of the alarming turn in the affairs of their country. So it had come, the thing which he had feared for some time now. Turning to Barbara, he said quietly, "Don't be so alarmed, dear wife. You know I could never go and kill my fellowmen. But if we are compelled to go, remember that God will take care of you and the children."

"Yes, Johann, He will, I know, but tell me, did you know anything of this war? Had you heard it was coming?" she questioned her husband.

"My dear Barbara." His voice was very tender, and as he placed his right arm protectingly about her shoulders, he said frankly, "Tis true, I have heard some talk of late that a revolution was feared, but I did not want to worry you. I was hoping and praying that it would not come to pass. Now that it has come, we can only wait and pray. God has never failed us; He will not fail us now," he added with a note of surety in his deep voice.

# CHAPTER

## 2

It came the next evening, the thing they had feared and dreaded. And yet they were not prepared for it—so rudely was their peaceful home life interrupted.

Johann and the boys were washing for supper. Barbara placed a steaming bowl of vegetable soup on the table and began cutting slices from a loaf of bread.

Annie drew the chairs up to the table.

Baby Elizabeth was already sitting on her own little stool, impatiently waiting for her supper.

A sudden loud rap on the door startled them all. Barbara caught her breath sharply. Johann straightened his shoulders, went to the door, and opened it. In the gathering dusk of the summer evening, he saw a man in full uniform, an officer of the law.

"Man of the house, I presume?" the caller gruffly inquired.

"Yes, sir, I am." Johann spoke quietly but clearly.

"Well, then, war is on, you know, and we want every man that can shoot a musket at once! Be at Edwardsdorf at the square,tomorrow morning at 8:00 o'clock sharp." The man barked his orders.

"I'm sorry, sir, but I cannot take up arms. It would be wrong for me to do so, according to the teaching of the Bible." Johann spoke firmly and with deep conviction.

The officer swore and said sneeringly, "So? You're another one of those _____ cowards. I met one up the road awhile ago." He pointed in the direction of the Kauffman home. "If you fail to appear in the morning you will both meet the same fate—you will be shot to death. Make your own choice." He turned abruptly, sprang on his waiting horse, and galloped away.

Johann stood watching for a moment. Then as the sound of the horses' hoofs died away, he closed the door. The frightened children had drawn close to their mother, little Annie trying to hide behind the folds of her mother's skirts. Now they began to sob and crowd around their father.

"Be calm, dear children," Johann said, trying to comfort them. "Peter and Joseph, you are my big boys, and you will need to be brave and help Mother all you can until this is over."

"But Father," Joseph wanted to know, his big blue eyes wide and fearful, "what will they do to you at Edwardsdorf?"

13

"That, my son, we do not know." Johann placed his big strong hand gently on the blond head of his eldest son. "God is our refuge and strength, a very present help in trouble," he quoted reverently.

No one had much appetite now. The desire for food was forgotten. Supper was nearly cold, yet the wise parents realized that the children must be fed and that they too must try to eat. They would need extra strength for the days ahead. Barbara somehow managed to get through the meal, eating very little.

It was the custom of the Strauss family to read a chapter from the Bible before retiring. This Bible was one of their dearest treasures. Belonging at one time to Barbara's grandparents, who had fled from one country to another, it had been carefully carried along with their few cherished possessions.

Johann opened it tonight to the beautiful Twenty-third Psalm. His voice was rich and mellow, and he read with deep feeling in the German language. "He leadeth me in the paths of righteousness for His name's sake." Yes, it was for Him they would be willing to suffer if need be. "Yea, though I walk through the valley of the shadow of death, I will fear no evil." The father read on to the end of the Psalm.

Then they knelt together in prayer and implored God's protecting care over them.

The children bade their parents goodnight and went to their beds.

Johann and Barbara still sat talking. There was so much to say and so little time. Was it to be their last night together?

Then Peter Kauffman came.

"No, thank you," he said when they offered him a chair. "I told Marie I would not be gone long. The officers were here too I suppose?" Johann and Barbara both nodded.

"I came to see what time we must start in the morning. It is a good two-hour walk, you know."

"Yes, we certainly do not want to be late," answered Johann.

They decided that half-past five would give them sufficient time in the morning to reach Edwardsdorf by eight o'clock, and Peter took his departure.

Shortly after, Johann and Barbara retired, once more committing themselves to the tender care of their heavenly Father.

Morning came, and the family rose early. While Johann and the children ate their breakfast, Barbara busied herself with packing a lunch for Johann. She herself couldn't eat. The very thought of food seemed to give her a choking feeling.

The time of parting came. Johann embraced each one of the children tenderly. Then, turning to his wife, who could not keep back the tears, he said comfortingly, "Be brave, dear one. We will meet again, God willing."

"Yes, Johann, I will try," she whispered bravely, and with a loving clasp to his breast and a kiss on her lips, the husband and father tore himself away.

Johann soon reached the Kauffman dwelling where Peter joined him after a similar parting

15

with his loved ones. The two friends talked as they walked rapidly along. Some time ago they had heard news that did not interest them at the time. This morning they talked of little else. It had become a subject of great importance now. The good Queen Catherine II of the Russian empire had extended an invitation to the Mennonite people to settle in Russia. Because they were a hard-working people and had the reputation of being good farmers, she desired them to teach her subjects their methods and thus help to promote better living conditions among her people. She promised, in return for their services, absolute freedom from participation in military service for a period of one hundred years!

But most of the Mennonites had been content to stay in Germany. The land was peaceable, and after much toil and effort they had succeeded in establishing homes. It was no easy matter to leave everything and begin over again, they well knew from their past experiences.

The two agreed now as they talked the matter over that the sudden plunge of their country into war would make their going to Russia impossible at this time.

At length they could see the tall steeples and the golden domes of the large cathedrals of Edwardsdorf. Approaching the designated meeting place, they noticed other Mennonites like themselves waiting nervously in the gathering crowd. There was their own beloved pastor Krehbiel. They nodded to one another in silent greeting.

The big clock on the steeple nearby slowly sounded out eight deep solemn tones. Several officers now came out of the building and commanded the men to enter and register. It took a long time to carry out this procedure. Johann and his companions of like faith stated their belief concerning war. They were gruffly told to wait in the next room until all were registered. During this time they seized the opportunity to eat the lunches they carried in their pockets. Their early breakfast, long walk, and tiresome wait had made them very hungry.

Towards sundown they, together with the entire group of draftees, were marched to the temporary army camp which had been set up about a mile northeast of Edwardsdorf. After a meager supper of coarse black bread, thin soup, and coffee, they retired for the night on the narrow, hard army cots, wondering what the morrow would bring forth.

They did not have long to wait. The following morning muskets were given out to the men. Peter Kauffman refused to take the weapon that was handed to him and said respectfully, "I'm sorry, sir, but I cannot take up arms. Please excuse me."

The officer in charge deliberated for a moment, then said shrewdly, "We'll soon take that out of you here," and to an officer of lower rank, "Put this fellow in the camp prison."

Peter was taken to an old, heavily-barred building where he was soon joined by Johann and the other brave men who for conscience sake stood so courageously for the right. They

17

wondered how long they would be kept behind those rough prison walls, yet withal their hearts welled up in gratitude and praise to God, for their lives had been spared, and they would willingly suffer, if need be, for His dear name's sake.

# CHAPTER

# 3

Life behind those rough walls became almost unbearable. The air was foul and rank because of the crowded conditions and poor ventilation. Their meals were brought to them but once a day. The bread was coarse and black and sometimes moldy.

Johann missed Barbara's good meals. He missed Barbara and the children. At times an unutterable longing to see them swept over him until it seemed almost more than he could bear. He prayed daily, yes hourly, that God would keep his hand over his loved ones.

It was a source of comfort to have dear Pastor Krehbiel in their midst. They spent much time together in prayer, and the minister spoke words of comfort and encouragement that cheered their burdened hearts.

There were those trying days when the officers would ask them again to take up arms. After their firm refusal, the food became scarcer until they began to fear it would soon cease altogether.

The days slipped into weeks. The hot August sun beat down unmercifully, and the heat and stench within increased.

Early one afternoon, the middle of the sixth week of their confinement, Johann's ears caught the sound of a distant rumble. Through a small crack in the wall, he saw a faint object moving along. As it came closer, he finally discovered it to be a wagon approaching. Soon he noticed another not far behind.

"I wonder if we are going to be taken away from here," Johann said to his companions, who by now were all aware of the approaching wagons.

"Anywhere, anything would be better than this place," spoke up Henry Muller quickly.

The clatter of horses' hoofs was now heard, and several burly-looking grim-faced officers rode up ahead of the wagons, dismounted, drew the heavy bolts, and swung the thick prison doors open.

"Into the wagons with you! We have fooled around long enough. It is high time you cowards are out fighting with the troops, and if you don't obey orders this time . . . " The head officer shook his big fist menacingly.

The men obeyed. It was a welcome relief to be out in the open and breathe the pure fresh air, warm though it was. Soon they were crowded into the two wagons. The drivers cracked their whips and they were off, the officers following closely in the rear.

They traveled the rest of the day, leaving the familiar country behind. Edwardsdorf's towers were no longer visible. On and on they went, over hills, along the banks of a river, across bridges. As the twilight shadows were falling, they entered a dark forest. The air here felt cool and refreshingly sweet to Johann and his friends.

Leaving the forest and rounding a curve in the road, they saw a big castle suddenly looming up before them, its outline silhouetted against the darkening sky. A new fear gripped their hearts. Perhaps they would be bound and left in this gloomy place to slowly starve to death! They soon learned, however, to their great relief that the deserted castle was to be their shelter for the night; and after their usual scanty fare they were shut up in one of the great foreboding rooms, there to sleep on the dusty floor, closely guarded all the while.

All the next day the heavy wagons lumbered steadily on. The men were weak from lack of food, and the rough ride was tiresome. Through villages they rode, over winding roads, sometimes stopping long enough to water the weary horses.

Toward evening in the outskirts of a large city, they came to a grinding stop in front of a group of buildings which were unmistakably army barracks. They saw wagons, like the ones in which they were riding, loaded with ammunition and supplies. They saw troops, heads held erect and muskets glistening in the fading sunlight, march into camp. Numerous officers were directing troops and commanding orders. Everywhere was the sign of activity. The tired men in the wagon were ordered out and herded once more into a guarded building. That night each was given a bowl of good thick soup in addition to the usual bread and coffee. How good the food tasted! It put new strength and hope into them. All except Johann and Peter. They lay quietly, side by side in one corner of the room, on the rough board floor. Neither of the two was able to sleep, though their bodies were very weary. The remark made by the officers when they left the prison near Edwardsdorf was still ringing in their ears. "It's high time you are out fighting with the troops," he had said, and they well remembered the look on his face as he shook his big fist emphatically.

"I fear for the morrow," Johann said softly. "I have a feeling something terrible is about to happen."

"So have I," Peter whispered back. "If we could only escape and somehow manage to get back home, maybe we could go on to Russia. But if we would get caught . . ." He shuddered in the darkness at the gruesome thought.

They lay quietly for some time, each thinking his own solemn thoughts. There was not a sound in the room, save the deep breathing of the men, all of whom seemed to be sleeping. Suddenly Johann raised himself up, resting on one elbow. He strained his eyes in the semi-darkness.

"What is it?" Peter wanted to know.

"This board under me seems loose," whispered Johann cautiously, and running his fingers along the edge, he discovered that it could be loosened altogether without much effort.

Then the two men made another discovery. The floor, they found, was a single one, and if they could coax one more board from its place, the opening would be large enough for them to slip through. By this time their hearts were beating high with excitement. Dare they think of attempting to make their escape? It all seemed so simple merely to slip through a hole in the floor, yet they would be taking a great risk, they well knew. But, they reasoned, if they stayed here, they would in all probability face death sooner or later.

The second board gave way, and the slight sound caused some of the men to stir in their sleep. Peter and Johann lay motionless a full ten minutes. Soon the regular, steady breathing of their comrades assured them that all was well. They both agreed that it would be wiser to escape unnoticed if at all possible, for when their absence would be discovered by the officers, the other prisoners could not be forced to tell what they did not know!

Their decision was made. Breathing a silent prayer to God for their safety, they turned to take a last look at their friends. The tears welled up in their eyes. Would they ever meet again? they wondered. They must act quickly now. Johann worked his way down through the narrow opening, slowly but surely. He succeeded. A few minutes later Peter joined him below. Then reaching up, they carefully put the boards back in place. Crawling on their hands and knees, they listened intently and stealthily crept out from under the building.

It was a bright moonlight night. Inside the dark room a few minutes before the two were not aware of this fact, and now the danger of being seen suddenly filled them with terror. Casting many anxious glances about them, they halted for a moment. It was then that they saw the guard! He was pacing slowly back and forth in front of the building from which they had just emerged. His back was turned. Now was their only chance.

The two fugitives glided softly and swiftly away from the army barracks. On and on they sped, never pausing in their flight to look around for any possible signs of pursuit. They headed by instinct for the heavy patch of timber that skirted the outer edge of the camp. Once the sharp crack of a twig startled them as they hurried along. They entered the woods; and a sense of elation filled them, yet with it a fearful feeling possessed them. Suppose they had been discovered!

They walked more slowly now, feeling safer in the concealing shelter of the dense forest. Weakened as they were, they realized that they must not over-exert themselves or they would be unable to go on. They soon found, however, that they dare not go deeper into the heavy timber lest they lose their way in its dark depths; so they made their way back to its

24

shadowy edge and continued their flight.

The first faint streaks of dawn were beginning to appear in the eastern sky when the two friends decided they must call a halt. They were almost at the point of exhaustion. Then too they dared not think of traveling by day. The danger would be too great. Where could they find a place of concealment?

Coming to the top of a little hill, they heard the noise of water in the valley not far below. They must try to reach the river. By following it they would be able to find their way much more easily through the unfamiliar country, and it would enable them to quench their thirst and to refresh themselves.

They directed their steps toward the stream. The descent was easier, and they soon found themselves on the banks of a small river where they drank deeply of the clear cold water and bathed their feverish brows.

Now they began searching for a hiding place. As if in answer to their prayers, Johann almost stumbled into a small dark cave. It offered them the shelter they so much desired. Thanking God for His watchful care, Johann Strauss and Peter Kauffman lay down in the back of the cave and were soon sleeping the sleep of utter exhaustion.

# CHAPTER

# 4

It was Sunday morning in Weirhof. The bright sun shone on the surrounding countryside, bathing everything in its warm golden glow. A small group gathered in the little stone church on this beautiful summer Sabbath morn. Their hearts were heavy with anxiety, and the women, children, aged grandmothers, and a few aged grandfathers united their prayers in behalf of the absent ones. They had just learned that their dear ones were in prison. Even their beloved pastor had not been excused, and the little flock assembled here felt that they were as sheep without a shepherd. They found comfort, however, as together they poured out their troubled hearts to God and committed their loved ones to His tender care. This time of anxiety and intercession for the safety of their loved ones knit the little group closely together and strengthened the bonds of Christian love between them.

The service ended, and after bidding their friends goodby, Marie Kauffman and Barbara Strauss, together with their children, set out for their homes. The children soon ran on ahead, and by the time the two mothers reached the Kauffman home, they were feeding the hungry, loudly quacking ducks.

Barbara turned to her friend and urged her to go on home with her to spend the rest of the day. "The children will enjoy being together, and the day will not seem so long and lonesome," she pleaded, and Marie gladly consented.

It did not take the two women long to prepare the simple meal, and as soon as they had eaten, they washed the dishes and tidied up the neat, colorful kitchen.

"Come out to my flower garden," invited Barbara. "It's cooler there and we can rest on the stone bench. The children are playing out there too, and we can keep an eye on them while we visit." She led the way to her favorite spot, a small stone seat in the shade of an apple tree.

Marie admired the beautiful flowers that grew in Barbara's neat flower beds. Then the two women seated themselves comfortably and settled down to visit. Their heavy hearts felt somewhat lighter since the service in the little church that morning, yet their conversation centered naturally on the burden that weighed so heavily upon them, that of their absent husbands. Oh, the terrible suspense of those long weeks when they had heard nothing from Johann and Peter and the others who had been compelled to leave their homes, and now at last the news had reached them that their loved ones were in prison.

The quietness of the afternoon was broken and their conversation interrupted when they distinctly heard the clattering sound of horses' hoofs coming rapidly down the road. Glancing fearfully at each other, the two women waited almost breathlessly as two riders and their horses swept into view. One glance confirmed their fears. The horsemen were officers in full uniform of the German army—big, heavy-set men with bushy mustaches and beards. Vaulting down from their horses, they came quickly up the path.

"Is this the Johann Strauss place? the man in the lead asked.

Barbara rose trembling from her seat. Her knees were shaking, and her legs were so weak she could hardly stand. "Yes, sir," she answered as calmly as she could.

"Come now then, where is your husband? Hiding, I suppose." Seeing Marie, he seemed to have a new thought. Turning questioningly to her he asked, "Are you Peter Kauffman's wife, and is that your house on down the road a piece?"

She nodded.

"Well, where are the scoundrels? You may as well tell at once. We have wasted too much time already looking for them, and we are in a hurry."

"But they aren't here. They have been gone ever since the war began, and we were told that they are in prison," Barbara tried to explain.

Oh, if they would only go now.

"Yes, they were there until a few days ago. Then they sneaked away one night, the cowards. But if we ever catch them . . ." the taller one threatened with an evil look in his eyes, leaving his sentence hanging unfinished.

His companion purposed to search the house, and they proceeded to do so without further delay. After looking in vain for the two men who they were so sure were hidden somewhere and leaving a trail of disorder behind in their frantic search, they directed their steps next to the little barn, coming out at last with disappointment and chagrin written plainly on their evil countenances.

Cold chills crept over the frightened women as they heard the oaths and curses fall from the lips of the officers, who mounted their waiting steeds and thundered away to search the Kauffman home.

\* \* \* \* \* \* \* \* \*

Towards midnight of the following day Barbara awakened from a fitful sleep. Ever since the officers' visit Barbara and Marie suffered untold anxiety. Where, oh where were Peter and Johann? Had the officers found them? At last Barbara drifted off into a troubled sleep. Suddenly she awoke with a start. The door was being opened quietly. She lay still and rigid as though paralyzed. Footsteps were coming nearer. Then she heard his voice, and Johann was bending over her.

"Johann, is it you?" she sobbed in her relief, clinging to him.

"Yes, dear wife, it is I at last," he answered.

"Thank God, the officers didn't find you then," Barbara responded gratefully.

"Were they here seeking for me?" he asked in great alarm. She told him all. Then Johann briefly and hurriedly related some of his experiences to her, adding, "And so, dear one, we have decided to try to go on to Russia, Peter and I, for to stay here would surely mean death."

"Oh, how can I bear to have you leave again, and so soon?" implored Barbara, rising and dressing in great haste.

"Never fear. You and Marie and the children must go too, but we cannot travel together, for Peter and I will need to travel fast and only by night. You can set out early in the morning, just as soon as you can get ready. And now I must tell you of a plan." He hesitated, knowing how hard this was going to be for her. "Peter and I have decided to take Elizabeth with us. She is too young to walk several hundred miles and much too heavy for you to carry."

Barbara nodded, her heart too full to speak. How could she bear to part with her baby too? How could a fifteen-month-old child do without its mother? But Johann was right. She could never carry the chubby Elizabeth on such a long journey. Yes, the men must take her with them.

Johann found a candle and lighted it, then quickly covered the windows so that its feeble rays would not be seen from without. They must

30

take every precaution for their safety.

Barbara hurriedly prepared some food for Johann and placed it on the table. As he ate hungrily, he told her that he had not tasted food since the day before when he and Peter had eaten some apples that grew on some seedling trees, along the roadside, and those apples had not been very filling to the two hungry men.

How thin and worn Johann looked! Barbara could hardly keep from voicing the thought aloud, but she could not trust herself to speak of that. Then she gently awakened the baby and with a heavy heart began to dress her for the journey.

Now the older children were roused from their sleep. They were overjoyed to see their dear father, but their joy was short-lived when they were told that he and little Elizabeth would soon be leaving them.

"We must hurry, for Peter will soon be here," Johann said, as he and Barbara finished tying the bundle of clothing firmly together. Another bundle containing food for the travelers was carefully made up. The amount of provisions for the long trip ahead was very small, it is true, but with a baby girl to carry besides, Johann knew that he could not possibly take more. The small sum of money, and it was pitifully small, Johann divided, generously leaving the greater share for his wife and children.

Drawing a crude map of the route over which they expected to travel, Johann gave Barbara the names of some of the villages and towns the families would pass through on their way to the Russian territory. He and Peter would follow the same route as closely as possible, although they would avoid passing through any towns.

They would wait for their wives and children somewhere on the outskirts of the Russian village, Kovno, which was just a few miles across the Russian border. Peter arrived. Once more, with hearts nearly breaking, not knowing if they would ever meet again, they fondly embraced and midst their tears bade one another farewell. Little Elizabeth was too young to realize the seriousness of the occasion, and she smiled sleepily as she snuggled close to her father's breast. One more last look at his dear ones and at the little home where they had all been so happy together, and Johann, with the little one in his arms, followed Peter out into the night.

It was a dark night heavy with shadows in spite of the fact that the sky glowed with the brilliance of stars that twinkled overhead. The men were thankful for that, for as long as they were in the immediate vicinity of their own homes, they would be in grave danger.

The chubby little one nestling so trustingly in his arms made Johann realize that her weight would soon tire the strongest man.

They passed a farm home, and the sudden shrill barking of a dog caused them to quicken their pace. Peter was carrying the sleeping child now.

On and on they walked until they were forced at last to stop for a brief rest; then resuming their march, they plodded steadfastly on. It was nearing dawn when they came within sight of the little village of Nordenburg. Both had been there a few times, but now they were aware that they must go no further today. Daylight was fast approaching, and the peasants were early risers. Where could the fugitives go?

To their left lay a field dotted here and there with newly made shocks of hay.

"The very place! We can hide ourselves in the hay," declared Peter, and Johann readily agreed.

Together they made their way among the fragrant mounds, and soon they were carefully concealed within two innocent-looking shocks of hay. Elizabeth was still asleep when Johann gently laid her down, and lying down close beside her, the weary wanderers were safe for the present, at least.

# CHAPTER

# 5

Early that same morning a little procession began wending its way down the quiet country road. Anyone who chanced to see the two sturdy young farm wives, their market baskets on one arm, bundles in the other, and six lively children prancing along ahead, would be almost sure to assume that the little group was on its way to market. However, a close observer would have noticed a serious expression on the sweet faces of the two women as they walked along.

That very morning they had said goodby forever to the little homes that were so dear to them. There had not been much time to gather together the few belongings they would be able to carry with them. Barbara had made sure the precious family Bible was packed carefully with the few other cherished possessions. Once more this Bible would go on a journey to a strange land. The food they would carry in their baskets. The cattle and chickens were turned out to find food for themselves. Saying good-bye to home wasn't easy. A wave of mingled emotions surged over Barbara when for the last time she looked around at the dear, familiar things she would leave behind. There was her spinning wheel in the corner. There was the big friendly stove, still warm from the fire she had kindled to prepare the morning meal. The big clock on the shelf ticked steadily away. Her favorite chair by the window called her thoughts to the ever-present knitting close by. She caught her breath with a sob as her eyes rested on baby Elizabeth's little stool. Where were Johann and her darling now? Last of all she noticed the cheerful, bright geranium on the window ledge, and the quick tears sprang unbidden into her blue eyes. Leave all this? Yes, for His sake she would.

They were ready to go now. Bravely they turned their faces away and started out on their long journey, traveling in the opposite direction from Edwardsdorf towards the little village of Nordenburg.

The morning air was fresh and sweet, the birds were singing joyously, and the children were delighted at the prospect of a long trip together. They trudged cheerfully along, each carrying a small bundle. Even the two little girls, Annie and Lena, carried small burdens.

They traveled on quite steadily, and noon found them a long way from their homes.

It was now the latter part of August; the early

morning coolness had gone, and the rays from the hot sun grew stronger on the little group of travelers. But they made no complaint, and having rested a little longer as they ate their lunch, they trudged on again, stopping to rest in the friendly shade of a clump of trees when they could or to quench their thirst if they were fortunate enough to find water.

Towards the middle of the afternoon they found a lovely spot to rest under the welcoming shade of a large oak where they lingered a little longer hoping that the hottest part of the day would soon be past. Then reluctantly they resumed their march.

They had traveled the distance from their homes to Edwardsdorf or to a neighboring village many times in this manner, yet it was a very weary, footsore little company that finally stopped to camp for the night. Their bed was the hard ground, their shelter the bright starry sky. Towards morning the heavy dew made them damp and uncomfortable. Their bones ached; their muscles were stiff and sore. Nevertheless, after a meager breakfast they started on again.

In spite of the many difficulties, they slowly gained ground. The children became fretful and begged to go back home. The temptation to yield was very great, but no, they dare not turn back now. Johann and Peter were somewhere ahead with little Elizabeth. Yes, they must go on.

For weeks they traveled steadily, their faces towards Russia. Their carefully rationed food supply was soon exhausted. They bought food when they came to a village, spending as wisely as possible, their money getting alarmingly scarce.

The month of August slipped away, and September came with its warm, sunny days. The days were still unpleasantly warm at times, but the nights were growing cooler. They must hurry on.

Sometimes they were fortunate in finding shelter for the night, several good-natured farmers allowing them to sleep in their barns. How comfortable and relaxed they felt as they lay stretched out in the thick soft hay in a barn loft! And how thankful they were that they had aroused no suspicions to be alarmed about!

There was that memorable night when, weary and dejected, their aching feet seemed too tired to take them further. Little Lena too, was not feeling well, and that increased their worries. They must find shelter tonight!

The welcome light of a farmhouse shone cheerfully in the dusky twilight. Barbara rapped gently on the door.

A large pleasant-faced German opened the door, staring in surprise at the forlorn little group before him.

"Could you possibly give us shelter for the night in your barn?" began Barbara. "The children are all tired, and this one little girl is almost ill," she added pointing to Lena.

The door was flung hospitably open. "In the barn, no—but in our house, yes. Come in. We have room for all of you, haven't we, Mother?" The good-natured farmer called to his wife.

That good woman now came forward saying, "Indeed, we do. Won't you sit down and rest yourselves? How tired you must be!" Her voice was full of genuine sympathy. Soon she was bustling about preparing supper for them. What a meal it was! The good hot soup was filling and delicious. The hungry, half-starved children smacked their lips. It was so long since they had eaten good, fresh, homemade bread. Then, wonder of wonders, there were fruit and little cakes! Even little Lena seemed to feel better already.

The two mothers told their new friends where they were going, why they had left their homes, and how they hoped to be reunited with their loved ones before too long.

The tender-hearted couple wiped the tears from their own eyes as they listened. They had heard of Mennonites, they said, and truly they must have a strong faith in God if they were willing to leave everything for His sake.

"Come now, you must go to bed. Tonight you shall sleep in beds," their kind benefactress told them, and they gratefully followed.

A good breakfast the next morning and the good wishes from their hosts saw the travelers set out with new hope and courage. They had covered the greater part of their journey now, and before many days they would reach the Russian Zone. Once there, Kovno was not far away, where they hoped to join their dear ones.

The little party stopped to rest by the side of a quiet, tiny stream. A big leafy tree offered them its cooling shade, and since it was nearing noonday, they chose this delightful place to eat the lunch the kind German lady insisted on packing for them that morning. Before long Joseph's sharp eyes spied someone coming down the road toward them. As the figure drew nearer they noticed something decidedly different in his appearance. Just what it was they couldn't quite make out. Perhaps he was a Russian. Then as he drew near them, he stopped. Marie and Barbara looked uneasily at the stranger, silently wishing that he would continue on his way.

Now he began to speak to them in their own German language, although his words had a strange accent. He had come from Russia, he said, and he was looking for just such a party as this, two women and six children who were on their way to Kovno. Were their names Strauss and Kauffman?

They answered him in the affirmative.

Well, then, now since he had found them, they were to go with him and he would lead them safely to their husbands who were anxiously awaiting their coming.

Their hearts were beating rapidly, and the two women hesitated. This was a critical moment. Dare they trust him, a perfect stranger? How could they know that he was not telling them a falsehood. Perhaps what they had heard a few months ago about Queen Catherine's promises to their people was untrue. Perhaps Peter and Johann were even now in prison and they would be taken also.

Sensing their feeling of distrust, the man now

reached in his pocket and drew out something, saying as he did so, "Would this help you to trust me?" He held up before their wondering eyes a little red apron!

"My baby's apron," Barbara sobbed, and clutching the little garment, she pressed it to her breast. She had made that little apron with her own hands. She would know it anywhere. Her mother heart yearned for her child after the long separation, and the sight of that little apron was almost more than she could bear.

"There, there," said the stranger kindly, the tears glistening in his own eyes. "You will soon see your little one again."

"But how—where did you get it?" asked the bewildered mother.

"Your husband took it off your little one the morning I left and sent it along in case you should doubt me. How good that he thought of this plan! Surely you will not be afraid to trust me now?" he questioned, yet knowing in his heart what their answer would be.

They gladly assented, and gathering up their belongings, started off once more, with Mr. Katosky in the lead. He had told them his name and more news of their loved ones. Their hearts were lighter than at any time since they had started on their adventure, and they joyfully anticipated a glad reunion soon. It was comforting to know that Johann and Peter and little Elizabeth had evaded the German officers and arrived safely in Russia.

# CHAPTER

# 6

Nearly three weeks before, two weary, foot-sore men, one with a little child in his aching arms, had tremblingly staggered across the line into the Russian territory. They were almost completely exhausted and in a dazed condition after their long, weary trek, but they had reached their goal at last. They were free! Kneeling there on the sod they poured out their thanks to God. No longer would they need to fear lest the German officers would suddenly come upon them. Overcome by their great weariness, they immediately fell asleep, only to be roused an hour later by the fretful cry of Baby Elizabeth. She was hungry, poor little one. Their food and money had been gone for some time now, and so for days they had been existing on a meager diet of berries and other wild fruits which had been very scarce indeed. Several times they had been forced to beg food from accommodating farmers for the sake of the little one.

Today, however, they had been unable to find food. This part of the country was wild and rugged, and villages and dwellings were far apart. They realized that they were facing a grave situation, for their own strength was fast failing. They must find food soon. One look at the child convinced them of that. Daylight was slowly fading, they discovered with some alarm, and tired though they were, they started slowly on again.

They had covered some distance, and the two friends felt ready to drop by the wayside when they caught sight of what appeared to be a village not far away. That must be Kovno. New hope filled their hearts. Surely they would find help there.

It was a balmy summer evening, but the weary travelers were barely conscious of the beauty around them as with slow, faltering steps they approached a dwelling at the outer edge of the village. The pleasant odor of food cooking drifted out to them. How good it smelled!

Several children who were playing in front of the cottage became frightened when they saw the strangers approaching and rushed into the house. A little later their father appeared in the open door where he stood waiting as the travelers came slowly up the path. He noticed their worn clothing, their untrimmed hair and beards, and the bundles they carried. His curiosity deepened when he saw the little child. He was sure they had come from afar, and their faltering steps gave evidence that they were almost to the point of collapsing. Greeting them in Russian, he invited them in, but their questioning look showed that they did not understand the friendly Russian who had spoken to them. He repeated his greeting in German, and although his words were somewhat broken, they understood him now and gratefully accepted the cordial invitation.

Frau Katosky left her place by the stove where she was preparing the evening meal. Stepping close to Johann, she gently took Elizabeth from her father's tired arms. The little one stared at the motherly woman's sweet face, then smiled and snuggled close to her soft bosom.

"She has missed her mother so, poor little one, and no doubt you remind her of her," murmured Johann compassionately.

In a few words he and Peter told of the long journey they had made from near Edwardsdorf, Germany, why they had left their homes, and then of the dear ones who were coming somewhere behind.

Frau Katosky had busied herself with feeding the famished child, and now that her hunger had been satisfied, the tired little head began to nod drowsily.

"Let me put her to bed. She can sleep in the cradle. Our Frederick has outgrown it. I will care for her tonight, if you will allow me," the good woman said to Johann, who willingly consented.

So little Elizabeth was put to bed as tenderly as if she were one of Frau Katosky's own little ones.

The food was then dished and put on the table for the family and their unexpected guests.

Peter and Johann were ravenously hungry, and they were quite sure that the strange new dish, which their friends called borsch, was the most delicious food they had ever eaten!

For over a week the men enjoyed the kind hospitality of the Katoskys. Their strength gradually returned, as they did little but rest and eat Frau Katosky's good meals. They wondered how they could ever repay these friends for their kindness. Their thoughts, too, were almost constantly of their wives and children. Surely the food had long since given out, and the money. If they could only go to meet them! But after talking the matter over it seemed wiser to wait where they were. The risk of returning would be too great.

That evening they were greatly surprised when Mr. Katosky proposed, "I will go to meet them and help them find their way. The villages, you know, are farther apart the nearer they get to Russia."

Peter and Johann were overjoyed to hear this proposal from the lips of their host, yet they hesitated to accept the generous offer.

"You have done so much for us already, and you know we are not able to pay you," Peter said regretfully.

"I want you to forget about that," Mr. Katosky replied. "You would do the same for me, I'm sure," he added, to which they both agreed.

"I heard you speak of some grain that needs to be harvested; perhaps we could do that for you," Johann suggested.

"Yes, I have a small field that was planted late in the spring. It is ready to cut now, but do you think you are strong enough to undertake such a strenuous task?"

Both men assured him that they felt equal to harvesting the grain, and so the agreement was made.

Early the following morning Mr. Katosky prepared to set out on his strange errand. How long he would be gone, no one knew. That would depend largely on where he would find the little band of travelers.

Johann's thoughts were troubling him. Would Barbara and Marie be willing to follow and trust a perfect stranger? It would be only natural for them to hesitate, he reasoned. Perhaps they would refuse. When he told the others of his fears they agreed that he was right. Why had they not thought of this before? They must think of a plan whereby the confidence of the two women could be secured.

Johann's eyes rested on his little daughter in Frau Katosky's arms. How sweet and fair she was this morning! Her cheeks were round and rosy again. Ah, if her mother could only see her now. Then a sudden thought came to him. Going over to his little girl, he took off her little red apron. Handing it to Mr. Katosky he said, "Take this little apron along and give it to her mother; she will surely believe and follow you then."

\* \* \* \* \* \* \* \* \* \* \*

The month of September was fast slipping away. There were still warm, sunny days—days when just a few clouds drifted lazily through the bright blue sky. There were others when a haziness reminded one that autumn was at hand. Harvest was nearly over. Men and women alike wielded the little hand sickles, cutting the golden grain and binding it into sheaves.

Johann and Peter enjoyed working in the fields. How glad they were that they had been able to carry on in Mr. Katosky's absence! Their former strength had returned, and they were able to spend long hours in the field. Little Elizabeth was happy and contented in the care of Mrs. Katosky. God had marvelously undertaken for them in all their wanderings, and they were confident that He would help them to establish homes in this land once more. When their families came, they would all go on together to Herodichtcz where they had heard some Mennonites had settled recently.

The next evening at sunset a little caravan was slowly wending its way toward Kovno. They were dreadfully weary, and were it not for their leader's encouraging words, they might have given up going any further that day. He had informed them that the first cottage they would come to was his, and there they would find their loved ones. As they came within sight of it at last, the three lads were suddenly filled with new strength and energy, and unable to bear the slow progress of the rest of the party, they ran on ahead.

Johann and Peter were sitting in the yard enjoying the fading sunset and the quiet tranquillity of the closing day. The Katosky children and Elizabeth were playing quietly in one corner of the yard. The two men were becoming attached to those well-mannered children. How Elizabeth enjoyed their company after being separated from her own brothers and sister! Ah, surely it would not be long now until they would be reunited, God willing.

So engrossed were the two fathers that they failed to see the little company so close at hand. They were sitting with their backs to the newcomers when suddenly they felt themselves seized from the rear. Warm arms were flung about them and boyish voices cried out, "Father, Father!"

What a glad surprise it was! The rest drew near, and the two families clung to each other, weeping out the tears of their long separation. Baby Elizabeth was clasped in her mother's arms in a close embrace, and all the pent-up tears flowed down Barbara's cheeks like rain. She had her precious baby in her arms again, Johann was there close beside her, and just now that was all that mattered.

Barbara reached out and patted the bundle that she had carried, and which Johann now held. The bundle contained some of her dearest treasures, and among them was a certain little red apron. One thing she was sure of—Elizabeth would not wear the little apron again. Barbara

47

would put it carefully away as soon as they had their own home once more. When Elizabeth grew up and had children of her own, she could show it to them and tell them how it had helped in reuniting her parents in a strange land.

# CHAPTER

# 7

The years glided rapidly by. It was springtime in Herodichtcz, and the leaves on the trees were beginning to unfold. The tender green grass was showing in the fields and along the banks of the river that flowed not far away. Early one beautiful morning, a horse-drawn wagon bumped along the road that left the pleasant little village and led through the meadows to the river. Riding in the wagon were several stout, cheerful farm wives and their daughters, rosy-cheeked young lasses, who were on their way to the river to do their family washings. Every two weeks they made the trip, spending almost the entire day in washing the soiled clothing that had accumulated during this time.

They reached the river bank, and after unloading their bundles, they all set to work. A fire was built under the large vats where the water was to be heated. Because there were no matches in those early days, flint was used to obtain sparks, and much care and patience were required to kindle a fire in this manner. The water was carried from the river, the sturdy, younger women usually taking care of this strenuous task.

The bundles of clothing were taken down to the water's shallow edge where they were put to soak for a time. Then with strong homemade soap, the women rubbed the soiled garments and beat them upon the rocks, back and forth, repeating the process over and over until they were satisfied that every particle of dirt was loosened. By this time the water in the vats was boiling. Into these steaming receptacles the clothes were dumped, and more soap and lye were added. Then with long sticks the women stirred the clothes from time to time, later lifting them out and taking them to the river again, this time to rinse until clean and snowy white. Some of the drudgery was taken out of the task, as together they worked and exchanged pleasant conversation in a friendly and intimate manner. Occasionally a merry laugh rang out on the morning air.

Elizabeth Strauss, her sleeves rolled up to her elbows, was busily engaged in rinsing the clothes in the clear cold water. Up and down, up and down, she dipped them, then with a deft turn of her right hand wrung the water from them.

At eighteen Elizabeth was a very attractive young woman. Her blue eyes revealed a depth of character, and her waving blond hair was neatly braided and wound around her head. She

50

sang softly as she worked.

This lovely spring morning Elizabeth was especially happy. And why shouldn't she be? Just last evening, and Elizabeth still thrilled to the memory of it, Peter Graber had asked her to be his wife, and she had consented. In sharp contrast to Elizabeth's light hair and fair skin, Peter's complexion was of a darker hue, and he possessed a head of shining black hair. But most important of all was the assurance that Pete, as his friends called him, was a sincere Christian. Her parents, too, did not object to the choice their daughter had made.

"Why so happy, Elizabeth? Was Pete over to see you last night?" teased Carrie Senner, her best girl friend.

Elizabeth blushed a little, dropped her eyes a moment, then shyly replied, "Yes, Carrie, and if you promise you won't tell, I'll tell you a secret."

Carrie quickly promised and Elizabeth whispered the words softly in her friend's ear.

"Elizabeth Strauss, you are a lucky girl!" exclaimed Carrie in a low tone, adding sincerely, "Pete is a fine fellow, and I hope you will be very happy together."

"Thank you, Carrie. I know we shall, for we both feel that God has led us together," she answered, her eyes glowing with happiness.

The girls finished rinsing the clothes, and gathering them up, they joined the others on the river bank where they spread the clothes on the bushes to dry.

It was now past noon day, and having finished

their washings, the group sat down on the grass to enjoy the lunches which they had brought along.

While they waited for the clothes to dry, the women and girls did not dream of sitting idle, and now each drew out her handwork. Soon they were all engaged in knitting, mending, or sewing of some sort. Thus employed, the afternoon was spent pleasantly, and though their hands were busy, their bodies rested after their strenuous work of the morning.

When the clothes were dry, they were neatly folded and bundled together for the trip home. Today Tena Muller was driving her father's team, and the horses which had been tethered close by were hitched to the wagon by the young girl. Presently the group was on its way back to the village. Washing was done for another two weeks!

True to her word, Queen Catherine II had furnished these simple, devout Mennonite people with materials to build homes for themselves and had supplied them with farming tools and other necessary items. She had also exempted them from military service. This exemption was of great importance to them because of their strong belief in nonresistance. Although they were required to learn to speak the Russian language, they were permitted to converse freely in their own native tongue.

Herodichtcz boasted only one long street which ran the entire length of the village and was bounded on both sides by the homes of the villagers. Each little house was joined by a small barn, with a shed between. Back of each set of buildings was a narrow strip of land. While Mennonites did not own their homes, they were allowed to live there, and in return they spent most of their time teaching the Russians their methods of farming, devoting the little time they had left to the small plot of land which had been granted to them for their own use.

Flax was one of the chief grains which they raised. After threshing and various stages of processing, it was woven by the women into linen cloth.

Their only source of dye was onion skins, the bark of the red oak, and other natural resources, which provided a limited variety of color for their cloth. Thus most of the clothing worn, and especially the shirts and trousers of the men, were white. No wonder they had to be washed so thoroughly on wash day.

The day was drawing to a close, and the sun's last rays were disappearing behind the distant hills when the wagon and its occupants drove into the village. One by one, the women and girls alighted from the wagon, taking their bundles with them. When they reached the Strauss home now, Elizabeth helped her mother down.

"Goodbye, Tena, and many thanks," they called.

Tena gaily waved her hand in farewell and turned the horses in the direction of home.

The mother and daughter entered the house together. Barbara sat down and began to sort the clean-smelling clothes.

"What a nice day we had to wash and dry the clothes!" she commented in a tone of satisfaction.

"Yes, and the clothes smell so fresh and sweet," agreed Elizabeth.

The tinkle of many little bells now reached their ears. Elizabeth looked out the open door. Fritz, the herd boy, was coming home with the cows. Each morning he drove all the cows and sheep belonging to the villagers out to the meadow land to graze and brought them home again at night.

Elizabeth went to get the pail from its place on the bench, saying as she did so, "I'll put the cows in tonight, Mother, and do the milking. I know you are tired."

"That is very thoughtful of you, dear. I am quite weary tonight," Barbara admitted, adding with a little wistful sigh, "Oh, Elizabeth, I am going to miss you so much when you and Peter are married. Father and I will be alone then."

"I know, Mother, but I am not going to leave you for some time. I have some sewing to do, you know," she shyly replied, and stooping she placed a kiss lightly on her mother's forehead. Then she hastened out to meet Fritz who had arrived with the cows.

Elizabeth liked to milk. She loved to hear the pleasant tinkle of the bells and the contented munching of the cattle as they ate their supper of hay. With strong, capable hands, she was soon sending streams of foamy white milk into her pail.

At her work in the house, Barbara was smiling contentedly to herself. Elizabeth had always been a good, obedient daughter to Johann and her, she mused. Then her thoughts went back to the time when Elizabeth was hardly more than a baby and they had left their home in Germany, arriving at last in this country where God had allowed them to establish a home once more. The expression on her face changed to one of sadness as she recalled the hard experiences they had passed through, of the separation from her husband and child, of the many weary miles they had walked to reach this land they now called home. God had been good to them and answered their prayers. The children had all grown up and had homes of their own except Elizabeth, and soon she too would be leaving. Yes, Barbara was going to miss her!

\* \* \* \* \* \* \* \* \* \*

The wedding was over. Elizabeth and Peter were established in a home of their own. Elizabeth enjoyed her new role as housewife, for she was well acquainted with the arts of cooking, baking, soap making, milking, working in the fields, and doing numerous other tasks which occupied every minute of the day.

Baby John was born the next year. Of course the young parents thought he was the most wonderful child they had ever seen. As little John grew older, he became especially attached to his Grandfather Strauss. Elizabeth hoped and prayed that her little son would grow up to be a good man like her own dear father, whom she loved so well.

Christian was the second baby. He was a round, chubby little fellow. Four-year-old John was pleased and proud of his new brother.

Evenings were the most pleasant time of day, Elizabeth thought. The day's work in the field done, Pete was free to be at home with his little family. The young mother sat and sewed while Pete romped and played with the boys for awhile. Then a chapter from the Bible was read aloud by the father, after which they knelt together in prayer.

One cold snowy day in December their little girl was born. They named her Barbara after her grandmother Strauss. Little Barbara inherited her father's dark hair and dark eyes. How happy Elizabeth was at the coming of this wee baby girl! But she could not help wondering what the future held in store for the little one that nestled so securely in her arms.

Now Elizabeth was busier than ever, and she found it harder to manage her many duties, for after the birth of her baby girl, she did not gain her strength back so speedily as before.

One afternoon she and the children were visiting in the home of her parents. The children begged their grandmother to tell them the story of the "Little red apron." They never tired of hearing the story from the lips of their beloved grandmother, and it always touched their tender little hearts and brought tears to their eyes.

"Where is the little apron, Grandma?" young John wanted to know when the story was ended.

"Just a minute and I will show it to you," their grandmother answered as she left the room, returning a moment later with the faded little garment in her hand. The children looked at the tiny apron which their own dear mother had worn at the time the story had taken place and which meant so much to their grandmother.

Now the grandmother handed the little apron to her daughter saying, "Elizabeth, I have always intended for you to have this some day since it was yours, so I want you to take it now. You will never know how much I have treasured it," she finished brokenly.

Elizabeth gladly accepted the little garment from the toil-worn hands of her dear mother.

Only a few days after this incident took place, a great sorrow came into their lives. The dear mother and grandmother became ill, and in spite of all that loving hands could do, her gentle spirit took its flight at sunset of the following day. Her sudden passing was a great shock to her family and many friends and left an emptiness behind.

"Poor Father! How lonely he will be!" murmured Elizabeth when the funeral was over and their mother had been tenderly laid to rest.

"He shall come and live with us," offered Pete generously, and so for the next few years he made his home with them. Later he went to live with his oldest son, Joseph, where he stayed until his death several years later.

When little Barbara was seven, the Grabers welcomed their fourth child, a son whom they named Jacob. For several years now the young mother had not been strong, and when their little son was born, the father was very anxious about his wife. It was the month of December, and the weather was bitterly cold when little Jacob arrived. Would the mother who was so near death's door recover? For several days her life had been in grave danger, and the father wept and prayed that God would see fit to spare Elizabeth's life, whom they all loved and needed so much in the home. But the tiny babe was only a week old when his sweet young mother slipped away to join her dear mother who had gone before.

# CHAPTER

# 8

Pete grieved much over the death of his young wife. What would he do now, with four motherless children, the youngest a helpless little babe?

Then Pete's sister, Mary Krehbiel, who had a family of five children of her own to care for, offered to take little Jacob for awhile, and so the sorrowing father consented. Seven-year-old Barbara, a bright little girl for her age, struggled along trying to keep house for her father and two elder brothers. Sometimes the women would spend a day helping the little girl with some of the harder tasks. Their help lightened the heavy load, yet Barbara missed her loving mother in the many long, lonely hours that followed, and often at night the little girl cried softly upon her pillow, longing for the dear mother who could not come back to her.

Katherina Senner was a strong, healthy girl of fourteen although she appeared to be much older. She often helped out in the Graber home, and Barbara clung to Katherina in her grief and loneliness. As time went on, Pete began to consider asking Katherina to be his wife. His children needed someone to mother them, and he longed to have his baby son at home. True, Katherina was very young, but she was so strong and capable that she would be well able to manage the affairs of the household and keep things running smoothly. It was not that he had forgotten Elizabeth so soon. Ah, no! Never would any other be able to take her place in his heart.

The following year they were married, and the young stepmother was only a year older than John, who was now fourteen. Year-old Jacob was brought home, and the family was together again.

During the cold winter months Barbara was often unable to sleep warmly in her bed at night. On these bitter cold nights the little girl would creep out of her bed and, shivering in the darkness, would climb on the broad chimney shelf behind the enormous brick stove. There she curled herself up and finally grew warm enough to go to sleep.

The care of little Jacob fell largely to Barbara besides the many household duties that were thrust upon her young shoulders. One of her daily chores was to carry water from the spring, which was back of the house on the slope of a little hill some distance away. With a yoke across her slight shoulders, from which two pails of water hung, the little girl staggered and sometimes fell under the heavy load. Needless to say she enjoyed few playtimes, and she was often so tired at night that she could hardly finish her tasks.

In the course of a year a baby girl was born whom they named Mary. Since Barbara had been the only girl in the family up to this time, she was very happy over the arrival of a baby sister although she knew this meant extra work for her.

Two years later Peter came. The family was growing, and Pete worked harder than ever to provide for them. John, now seventeen, had long been taking his place in the fields with the men. Christian and Barbara attended school in Herodichtcz when they were not needed at home.

Time passed rapidly by, and in October of 1856 another girl, Freni, was born. Barbara was now twelve and was developing into a strong, healthy girl as she approached young womanhood, and she was quite capable of performing the tasks that an older person would be expected to do.

At the age of fifteen an outstanding event took place in her life when she and several other young people sealed their Christian vows with water baptism. The sacred ordinance was administered by their bishop, John Schrag, and the solemn vows that she made that day Barbara purposed in her heart to keep as long as she lived.

Another year passed, and Joseph was born. That made eight children to cook, wash, and sew for in the crowded little house. There was little privacy under such conditions, and Barbara found herself longing, as any normal girl would for the time when she could have a home of her own. At sixteen, with her well-formed figure, clear skin, dark eyes, and hair as black and glossy as a raven's wing, she was indeed a wholesome and pleasing picture.

There was one young man who especially thought this to be true, and for some time now he had been admiring Peter Graber's eldest daughter. Joseph Schrag was a tall, broad-shouldered, heavy-set young man. His hair was a sort of sandy color with a faint reddish tinge, and his full beard took on an auburn shade. His family had emigrated to Russia from Austria for the same religious freedom that had caused so many others to leave their homes and find refuge in a new land. Joseph was very happy when this lovely young girl chose to accept his attention, and he soon became aware that she was a girl of unusual depth of character. Their courtship was filled with many rich experiences, and the more often they were permitted to be in each other's company, the more sure they were that they wanted to share life together.

Two years later they were married. The wedding day was set for February 6, 1864. A blanket of soft white snow lay on the ground, but the sun shone brightly on the little church where the relatives and friends of the young couple gathered to witness the ceremony.

In her simple wedding dress, Barbara had

never looked more fair, and her dark expressive eyes shone with a depth and earnestness rarely seen. Joseph stood beside her, tall and striking, and his voice came clear and strong as he spoke the marriage vows that would join them together for life.

"Oh, how wonderful it will be!" Barbara said happily to her young husband when they were settled in their own little home. "Just think, Joseph, a home of our very own." Her dreams were coming true at last.

"Yes dear, we shall be very happy here together." Joseph beamed down tenderly on his bride. How tall he was! How safe and secure Barbara felt in his presence!

The year following their marriage was indeed a happy one for the young couple. Joseph worked diligently, sometimes in the fields of the wealthy Russians nearby, sometimes in his own small plot of ground. Barbara busied herself with her household duties, doing her best to make the bare little home as attractive as she could, and she prepared tasty meals for Joseph when he came in tired and hungry from the fields.

One of their favorite dishes was borsch, a soup made of red beets, potatoes, and salt, with enough water to cook until tender; then vinegar and sour cream were added to bring out a delicious tangy flavor. They had learned to make this dish from their Russian friends, and it soon proved to be a favorite among them.

They also learned to make burega, another Russian dish that Joseph liked especially well.

This dish was made from a stiff dough of flour, salt, and water rolled very thin and cut into squares. A spoonful of cottage cheese, egg, salt and pepper mixed together was now placed on a square, which was then folded over and pinched tightly together. Next the squares were dropped into a pot of boiling water. When cooked thoroughly they were drained, and piping hot grease was poured over them.

Sometimes Joseph and Barbara would spend the evening visiting friends. On these occasions Barbara always took her knitting or sewing along, and if the neighbors lived close by, she often carried her spinning wheel with her. The two women would sit and visit happily together, their fingers busily at work, while the men in one corner of the room were exchanging thoughts, their tired bodies relaxed after a hard day's work in the fields.

In February little Jacob was born. The tiny son God gave them was a strong, healthy baby, and the young parents were very happy. Barbara loved to sit in her rocker and sing softly to her precious little boy. She was experiencing the tender joy of motherhood, and it was very sweet to her.

Little Jacob was only a week or two old when his parents first began to fear he was blind! They kept hoping and praying that their fears were false, but as time went on, they knew for sure that little Jacob could not see. It was a great disappointment to the young couple, but a greater disappointment was in store for them. At the tender age of thirteen weeks, the little one became very ill with pneumonia, and in spite of all they could do, the sightless eyes that had not been permitted to look upon the faces of his parents closed for the last time.

It was a sad and bitter experience for the young parents as they followed their baby to the cemetery where he was buried in the frozen ground, a little more than a year later than their wedding day. Little did they realize that this experience was only the beginning of the many hard trials and similar griefs they would face in the years that lay ahead.

Time rolled on, and God gave another son. They named him John. Little John was a husky baby, and the happy parents watched him grow and develop into a bright, healthy child. He soon toddled around, following Barbara as she went about her work, and his childish prattle was sweet music to her ears. Johnny, as he was affectionately called, became a winning little lad, with merry blue eyes and pretty auburn hair. Barbara was never lonely now, and Joseph, coming home at night and seeing the happy, contented look on her face, thanked God again and again for sending little Johnny to them.

When Johnny was four, sorrow again invaded their happy little home. For several days Johnny suffered with dysentery. His mother tried every remedy that she knew, but nothing seemed to relieve the little sufferer. He seemed to feel a little better shortly before midnight, and so Barbara yielded when Joseph urged her to lie down and rest. She must have slept for an hour when she was suddenly awakened. She sat up in bed. Oh yes, that must be Johnny calling to her. A feeling of remorse came over her. She hoped he wasn't worse!

"Mamma, I'm so hot," he called.

Barbara sprang out of bed and hurried over to where her small son lay. She placed her hand gently on his forehead, then drew it back hurriedly. The little head was burning with fever, and his breath was coming in short, quick gasps. She gave him a drink of water and quickly awakened Joseph. Together they ministered to their little son, trying to ease his sufferings. Then they began to fear that his life would be taken, and the young parents knelt by the bed where their only child lay, praying that God would see fit to spare his life, yet humbly resigning themselves to His sovereign will. Before the morning light dawned, little Johnny slipped away to be with his Maker and to join the little brother whom he had never seen.

Their hearts were bleeding. It was hard to give him up. But God sustained them in that dark hour and gave them strength to pass through the trying time. Someday they would understand why, but oh, how lonely and empty their home would be without little Johnny.

# CHAPTER

# 9

Barbara stood in the open doorway one warm spring evening. She breathed deeply of the invigorating air and feasted her eyes on the beauty of nature. Joseph would soon be coming home. Ah, there he was coming up the road now.

As he drew nearer, Barbara's keen eyes were quick to observe the worried look on her husband's face. She noted too that his steps lagged and lacked their usual buoyancy and that he seemed deeply engrossed in thought.

When he looked up and saw Barbara, the expression on his face changed, and a tender look came into his eyes. "How are you tonight?" he greeted her, his voice full of love and concern.

"Oh, Joseph, I am well, thank you, and the baby has been so good today," answered the young mother happily.

The tiny daughter whom God had given them was like a bright ray of sunshine. At six months little Mary was a plump, blue-eyed baby with soft, golden hair. Her small presence was a great comfort to Barbara, and the hours were no longer lonely since her coming.

Although Barbara longed to know what was troubling Joseph, she waited patiently, knowing he would tell her sooner or later. She had learned that long ago. So she finished preparing their simple evening meal while Joseph attended to the chores.

They sat on the front steps of their little cottage later, enjoying the twilight hour together. Baby Mary rested on her mother's lap, content for the moment. The fond parents talked of their little daughter's winning ways and recent accomplishments. Oh, how they hoped she would grow up to love and serve the Lord. Their faces were sober as they discussed her future, and this topic opened the way for Joseph to tell Barbara what had been on his mind all evening.

"Barbara," Joseph began a little abruptly, "Do you remember how and why our people came to Russia a good many years ago?"

"Why, yes, I heard the story often from my own grandparents. Their country was going to compel them to go to war, and of course since that was against the teaching of the Bible, they fled to this country because they were promised freedom here. But why do you ask? I'm sure you know this as well as I." She questioned anxiously as she looked up at him expectantly.

"Yes, dear, I know. I, too, heard it many times from my own grandparents, but conditions here are changing, and it may be that we too will be facing the same situation. The rulers are threatening to take away the guarantee that was granted our people these many years, and we must begin at once to make plans for the future." Joseph made an effort to remain calm.

Barbara clasped her baby tightly. "Oh, Joseph, is it really true?" Her voice was filled with distress. This, then, was what was troubling Joseph. No wonder he had hated to break the news.

"Yes, dear, but don't worry." He laid his big hand over hers protectingly. "The same God that our grandparents served is just the same today. And He is just as able to see us through whatever may come. Now I want to tell you something." He spoke slowly, choosing his words carefully. "Today several of us talked the matter over while we were at work in the fields. We have decided to try to go to America."

"To America!" echoed Barbara. "Oh, but that is so far away, and besides it would cost a great deal to go there, wouldn't it, Joseph?" Tears filled her eyes at the thought.

Joseph stroked his beard thoughtfully. "Yes, indeed, America is a long way from here," he agreed, "but think what it would mean to us—to little Mary and all of the coming generations. If we want to enjoy religious freedom, we're going to have to go where it is allowed. Then, too, America is a land where we could own our homes and work for ourselves." His voice had risen with animation, and he continued, "As for the cost, you are right, Barbara. It would take quite a sum to secure a passport to America, and if we decide to go, we shall have to skimp and save in every way possible."

Barbara sat silently wondering how they could manage to raise such a large sum of money when it was all they could do now to make a living. As for luxuries, they were used to doing without them. But if Joseph thought it was possible, she would do all she could to try to save even more, and she bravely told him so.

The other Mennonite families in the village faced the same problem. Many of them had large families to support. Among these were the Peter Grabers, whose family had increased until there were now twelve children, although the three oldest were married and had homes of their own.

One evening the group met to discuss plans for the future. War clouds were threatening, and they needed to act soon. It was unanimously decided to send one of their group over to America to thoroughly investigate the advisability of the planned emigration. He would also contact Mennonites who had previously settled there and look for possible places of settlement. Now another important question confronted the group. Who would qualify for this great undertaking? In the end, after serious thought and much prayer, John Schrag was delegated to take over this great responsibility. He was a great uncle to Joseph, an older, mature man, and had always been an acknowledged leader in their group. They felt he would act wisely in the momentous step ahead.

Accordingly, John Schrag sailed for America as soon as the necessary arrangements could be made, the whole group helping to bear the expense of the long journey across the sea. They hoped the war would hold off until Uncle John could return from his mission. God heard their prayers, and the tense war situation cleared for a time.

Two years passed. Another little daughter, Fanny, came to gladden the home of Joseph and Barbara. This little one had dark eyes and hair like her mother.

Joseph worked early and late. Occasionally he found odd jobs whereby he earned a few extra rubles. Barbara did her share too, making some extra butter and cheese from the milk their cow provided, then taking it to Kotusowka to sell. This was a larger town where they did most of their trading. Sometimes Barbara did some housework for a wealthy Russian lady, but with two little girls to care for, she found it hard to get away.

In the meantime Uncle John returned from America. He was enthusiastic about his recent trip and told glowing stories of the land across the sea. There were many opportunities there, he said, but he reminded them that they must not forget their real reason for leaving their homeland. They must remember that their motives in going were for their spiritual welfare, and material gain would be only secondary. They knew he was right. The desire to go to America burned anew in their hearts, and

Uncle John too was eager to begin to actually make preparations for the emigration.

Joseph purchased a large trunk at Kotusowka, and the day came at last when Barbara began to wash, mend, and pack their clothing. She packed and re-packed, trying to make room for the clothes and other precious articles they did not want to leave behind.

The household furniture, of which there was very little, the chickens, stock and other possessions were sold, and their sale helped to swell the little fund so carefully saved. The wagon and horses, however, would be needed for transportation to Lenburg before being sold. At Lenburg the emigrants would board the train.

Sadness tugged at their hearts when for the last time they gazed at the dear little home here they had shared life's joys and sorrows together. Barbara stood staring. In the distance she could see the dim outline of a little knoll where two small graves lay. Her own dear mother rested there too, also her grandparents, Joseph's parents, and others who had been near and dear to them. She turned her brimming eyes away. It was hard to leave them and go so far away. Joseph sought to comfort her, gently reminding her that some glad day they would all meet in that home above.

Nightfall found the group of men, women, and children boarding the train at Lenburg. The first lap of their long journey had begun. They would go by train through the western part of Russia, across the greater part of Germany to the large seaport Bremerhafen, where they would sail for America.

Barbara was glad they were not going alone to the new land. Her parents, the Peter Grabers, her two married brothers and their families, Joseph's brothers and sisters, were among the group who were emigrating. The train ride was a new experience for both old and young. Bright-eyed, four-year-old Mary took in the interesting sights along the way, and her active mind prompted her to ask innumerable questions. It proved to be a long, tiresome journey, however, before they reached their destination, and the steady click-click of the train wheels became monotonous. At night they tried to sleep, but the seats were crowded, and their bodies became very weary. After days of traveling, the whole group was thankful when they reached Bremerhafen. Collecting their bundles and trunks, the band of Mennonite emigrants found lodging at a large hotel where they could stay until their passports were purchased.

At last, on the first day of June, 1874, they approached the harbor where the CITY OF RICHMOND, a large sailboat, lay anchored. Soon they found themselves walking up the gangplank that led to the deck. Their hearts were filled with mixed emotions as the boat was loosed from its moorings. The sailors hoisted the big sails, and the great boat slowly began to move. As the land faded from their view, they realized that they were separating perhaps forever from their native land. The boat rocked on the crest of the waves as they sailed further out into the sea. Ah, they must not be afraid, yet they knew that many a ship never reached the port for which it was bound.

As Barbara stood with her family near the ship's railing, she was reminded of a phrase her grandfather often quoted when relating his experiences in prison and on their flight to Russia many years ago. "For His Name's Sake," he had reverently quoted. Now as she thought of the words, they seemed to fit this situation too, and she felt greatly comforted. She was a child of God, and she would not be afraid!

# PART 2

# CHAPTER

# 10

The big sailboat ventured slowly westward, ploughing its way steadily through the heavy sea. Many times the wind was not in their favor, and their progress was hindered. There were times too when severe storms came up and the strong gales blew the ship away from the charted course. As the boat rocked helplessly about in the treacherous sea, waves dashed over the deck, drenching living quarters and belongings. The lurching of the boat brought added discomfort to those who suffered from seasickness. Along with these hardships, the passengers found their quarters cramped and uncomfortable and the days monotonous. The food was carefully rationed. Would it hold out until they reached America?

No one knows the hopes and fears within the hearts of those numbered in the brave little emigrant band making the perilous voyage. The hardest trial came when death claimed two of their number. It was then they fully realized how much their faith in God meant. The faith that had prompted them to leave home and friends would also carry them through their sorrow. With this assurance their hearts were comforted, knowing that they had nothing to fear in life—or death.

For nearly two months they sailed along in this manner. Those on board grew weary and eager to reach their destination. How good it would be to set their feet on firm soil again!

At last one day about noon the captain announced joyfully that land had been sighted. New York harbor was not far away. Needless to say, there was great excitement on board. The good news brought renewed energy and revived spirits. The travelers strained their eyes trying to get a view of their new homeland.

July was nearly gone. The air was warm and sultry with little breeze stirring. Never had the boat seemed to move so slowly! But the sea was smooth and calm and the sailing pleasant as they glided toward the harbor. They moved so slowly that darkness was settling down over the land when the CITY OF RICHMOND finally entered the channel and docked at the pier. While the crew dropped anchor and busily attended to their assigned duties, the little group of Mennonites thanked and praised God for bringing them safely to America. The future was before them, an uncharted course. They were entering into a new life in a new land, and the way was unknown. Yet they could go on with confidence, for God was with them.

Because of the late hour of arrival, everyone remained on board that night. The sky glowed from the beautiful lights shining over the great city, and their reflections mirrored in the water fascinated the emigrants who were getting their first close glimpse of the new land. A cool breeze began to blow, and it was pleasant on deck after the heat of the day.

Joseph Schrag and his little family stood at the rail with others of their group watching the scene before them. Little Fanny was in her father's strong arms. Mary clung to her mother's hand, gazing in awe and wonder at the beautiful sight. They stood for awhile in silence, many thoughts going through their minds. Here was the land that was offering them freedom and liberty. After leaving New York, they would settle farther west. They hoped to join others of their faith who had already established homes in this country some years before. It is true there would be many adjustments for the newcomers since everything would be new and strange. In a day or two the group would separate, and this would create a new difficulty—the language problem. Uncle John had acquired a limited knowledge of the English language on his first trip to America, and they were glad they could rely on his help during the coming days.

Barbara sighed softly. Oh, how weary she was! She thought again of the home far away in Russia, of the dear familiar surroundings they had left behind, and wondered if they had done right in making this venture after all.

Joseph heard the faint sigh and looked down into the sweet face of his young wife. He suddenly became aware that her pretty dark eyes were sad and dull, and her usually rounded cheeks were thin and lacking their rosy color. He touched her shoulder gently. "You are tired, aren't you, dear? I hope it won't be long until we can settle down and you can get some rest." His voice was full of concern.

Barbara looked up gratefully. What a comfort Joseph was! His loving words fell like a healing balm on her troubled heart. A trusting warmth flooded over her. "Oh, Joseph, you are right. I didn't know I was so tired. How good it will be to have a little home of our own again." And in the deepening twilight her husband noted happily that her eyes were bright and glowing and her face wore a new look of contentment.

The next morning an eager, yet bewildered, little group prepared to leave the boat that had been their home for several months. With Uncle John in the lead, they streamed down the plank that led to the shore of their new homeland. They had been warned to keep close together. Fathers grasped the hands of their young children tightly as they hurried along the unfamiliar streets of the big city. Mothers pressed their babes closely to their breasts. Already they were seeing strange new sights, and waves of mingled emotions swept over the group as they made their way toward the train depot.

The depot was a busy place with many people milling about. Surrounded by their trunks and baggage, the group of Mennonites waited for

78

the trains that would take them to their various destinations. Many of their faces bore traces of sadness, for the thought of the separation ahead brought sorrow to their hearts. The close companionship of the past few months had formed a deep intimacy that welded them closely to each other. But part of the group had decided to go west to the Dakota territory, a newly settled section where some of their people had settled previously. Others wished to go to Kansas where they too planned to join relatives and friends. Still others decided to locate in Ohio. Among this last group were the Peter Graber and Joseph Schrag families.

Joseph longed to be among those bound for the Dakota country. His heart had been stirred with an intense longing to see this vast prairie land. He had been told of the great opportunities awaiting those who were brave enough to pioneer there. But unfortunately, their savings had dwindled to a small sum, and the Schrags felt God was leading them to Ohio for the time being. Joseph hoped to find work there, and he consoled himself with the thought that as soon as they could save enough money, they too would go to Dakota, God willing.

It was the forepart of August when the Grabers and Schrags arrived by train at Columbus Grove, Ohio. Here they were warmly received into the homes of the few Mennonites living there. The comforts of home life were a real treat after the long ocean voyage and tiresome train ride from New York.

Their arrival was timed just right, for the

threshing season was in full swing. Joseph soon found employment with Mr. Swartz, a Swiss farmer. Since the language of his employer was similar to the German, the two got along well. During the busy season Mrs. Swartz had extra hired hands to cook for, so Barbara was engaged to help her. This arrangement was ideal for the young couple, and they happily set up house-keeping in a little log cabin belonging to Mr. Swartz. They could not help but marvel at the way God was providing for their needs in this new land.

For nearly a year, the Schrags worked faithful-ly for the congenial Swiss family. By this time they had become so attached to their kind employers that it was hard to think of leaving. In spite of this contentment, Joseph could not erase from his mind the desire to go to Dakota. Uncle John had told him repeatedly in recent letters of acres and acres of prairie land waiting for some-one to claim them. To Joseph, who had never owned even the smallest plot, such a possibility was almost unbelievable. It was no wonder his heart burned with desire to go and see for him-self the picture Uncle John had painted so vivid-ly. He thought again of the conditions that had brought about their emigration from Russia. As he looked back and remembered all they had left behind, he was glad they had been able to break away from the rigid rules of the Russian empire. Yes, God had marvelously undertaken in their behalf, and Joseph prayed they would have His leading in the next step they were considering.

Barbara shared Joseph's dreams, and together they managed to save a good share of their earnings. They began making plans to leave for the Dakota territory, and late in July they boarded the train for the land of their dreams.

As the train sped on its way, both of the young parents realized that the step they were taking was a serious one. They knew that the life of a pioneer was not easy, but they were both young and strong and full of enthusiasm. Along with these qualities, they shared a deep concern for the welfare of their children, and their desire was that they might be able to provide for them both physically and spiritually.

Several days of traveling brought them through some thickly settled areas of prosperous farming country. Then the scenery began to change. The farms were becoming widely scattered and the country wild and barren. They rode for miles and miles through long sections of flat prairie land with only an occasional farmhouse miles away from its nearest neighbor, standing bravely on the plain.

Five-year-old Mary and Fanny, now three, were enjoying themselves immensely. There were so many sights to see! There were numerous lakes along the way, and the water glimmered in the bright sunlight. The sky was a beautiful blue, bluer than Mary's lovely deep blue eyes. Now and then a flock of birds rose from the edge of a lake as the train went rushing by.

At last they crossed into Dakota territory.

Joseph felt his pulses quicken. It wouldn't take long now to reach Yankton where Uncle John had promised to meet them. They could hardly wait to see him. He was always so jolly and good-natured, and he dearly loved to tease.

The train began slowing down. The passengers began to gather their things together as they came to a stop. It was in the middle of the forenoon, and they had reached Yankton.

Several teams were tied to the hitching post near the station, and almost before the travelers knew it, Uncle John appeared.

"Hello, everybody!" was his hearty greeting. He grasped Joseph's outstretched hand and greeted Barbara and the girls warmly. "My, how you two have grown! " he exclaimed, hugging Fanny and tweaking Mary's ear. "Won't Aunt Lizzie be surprised? Well, we better get started; we have about thirty-five miles to go." He rubbed his hands together briskly and started towards the wagon.

When their baggage and big trunk were loaded into the wagon, they all climbed in and found seats. Uncle John spoke to the horses, and they were off.

The team jogged steadily on. Once in a while they passed a homestead as they followed the dim wagon trail over the prairie. As far as they could see, there were wide open spaces about them. How different this country was from what they had been used to, and how fortunate they were to be here at last!

Joseph and Barbara were eager to hear news

of their friends here in this newly settled country, and Uncle John, too, had many questions concerning the relatives in Ohio. He was glad to hear that Barbara's parents, the Peter Grabers, were also planning to come to Dakota in a year or two.

Barbara glanced at the little girls and smiled tenderly. They had fallen asleep, their heads pillowed on the bundles beside them. The murmur of the grownups' voices and steady creaking of the wagon had lulled them to sleep. She didn't blame them, for she was very tired too. She wondered how much farther it was to Uncle John's house.

The faithful horses plodded on. Finally the sun began to sink in the west, and twilight settled quickly over the land. One by one the bright stars came out and twinkled overhead. Uncle John urged the horses on. He and Joseph talked companionably together. Barbara's eyes became heavier and heavier.

She must have slept a little, for suddenly she awakened and heard Uncle John saying, "Well here we are; welcome home!"

The wagon rolled to a stop in front of a little sod house.

Home! What a sweet word it was to Barbara's ears. She rose stiffly from her seat, and Joseph helped her down.

In the doorway Aunt Lizzie's ample form appeared barely visible in the feeble lamplight. She called out a cheery greeting, and, the next minute Barbara found herself folded in loving arms in a warm embrace.

"Oh, it's so good to be here," Barbara told her gratefully.

The little girls were wide awake now, and they climbed down with Uncle John's assistance. In the light of the kerosene lamp, Aunt Lizzie held the girls away from her after she had given them each a hug and kiss. "I want to see how much you have grown. Ach yes, just as I thought—how big you are getting to be!" She beamed as she bustled away to draw up a rocker for Barbara. "Here, sit down and rest your weary bones; you must be about worn out with all your traveling," she murmured sympathetically. Going over to the big shiny black stove, she threw in a handful of chips. "You should have something to eat and then go straight to bed!" she declared.

Barbara needed no second invitation, and sinking down gratefully into the comfortable chair, she looked about her. The room served as both kitchen and livingroom of the little sod house. The kerosene lamp in the center of the table gave a soft, cheery light. On one side of the room stood a bed covered with a spread of colorful calico print. At the other end of the room hung curtains of the same cheerful print, behind which was a tiny bedroom. The bare earthen floor was worn smooth from constant use and energetic sweeping of Aunt Lizzie's broom of prairie grass. It was all so pleasant and home-like that Barbara found herself longing for the time when they too could be settled as cozily as Uncle Johns. She hoped it would be soon.

Aunt Lizzie took a pan of delicately browned biscuits from the oven when the men came in from the barn. How good everything smelled! A big kettle of beans simmered on the back of the stove, and there were fried potatoes, beef, and rich brown gravy. A dish of stewed wild plums sat in the center of the table.

The men washed in the tin basin on the bench by the door. Then they combed their hair and smoothed their full beards. Uncle John laughed a good deal and joked good-naturedly. His laugh was always contagious, and soon everyone joined in the merriment as Aunt Lizzie put the finishing touches on the meal and called them all to supper.

With heads bowed reverently, Uncle John asked the blessing on the food. He thanked God, too, for bringing their loved ones to them safely, and in their hearts Joseph and Barbara echoed a fervent amen.

# CHAPTER

## 11

For nearly six weeks the Schrag family stayed with Uncle Johns. It is true the little sod house was crowded, but Aunt Lizzie didn't seem to mind sharing her home with another family. "You are welcome to stay as long as you like!" she declared hospitably. "Besides, where else would you go?" she questioned, and they knew she was right. Joseph had been so busy he hadn't found time to look for a claim, and they had no other place to stay.

On the first day of August, their third daughter, Anna, was born. When the excitement of the new arrival was over and life settled back to normal, Barbara was more eager than ever to get settled in a home of their own. But she was grateful that Joseph had found work soon after their arrival in Dakota. Every cent would be needed when they were ready to start housekeeping again.

Joseph, along with Uncle John and other

farmers, worked early and late in the fields. After the grain was cut, the bundles were put in shocks to cure. Then followed the threshing. One of the older, more well-to-do settlers had purchased a remarkable new machine invented to thresh grain. The new invention proved to be a wonderful labor-saving device. All the farmers were eagerly awaiting the day when the crew would arrive to begin work in their fields.

Joseph enjoyed his work. Although he had seen one of the machines operate in Ohio, he still marveled at the efficiency of the new invention. Run by horse power, the machine could accomplish a great deal in one day. The bundles of grain were pitched into the yawning mouth of the separator where through some remarkable process the grain was separated from the chaff and straw all in one operation. How different from the old homeland way of threshing in Russia! There it took many days to thresh out that amount of grain with their flails by hand. Yes, indeed, this was a great country!

The days sped swiftly by. The men put in long hours from daylight until dark. Then came the last day when the crew wound up their work for the season at Uncle Johns. Barbara and Aunt Lizzie served dinner and supper to the hungry men. How their English neighbors enjoyed the good meals! It was dark when the last man drove away with his team. Joseph breathed a deep sigh of relief; now that threshing was over, he could see about finding a claim.

At the first opportunity he and Uncle John set

out to look for land that was available for homesteading. Tramping over the prairie, they spent hours searching for a claim that would be suitable in every way. Two important factors considered essential by most claim owners were water and good grazing for their stock. About one and one-half miles from the little station Marion Junction was a quarter section of one hundred and sixty acres that appealed to Joseph. Running through this section was a fair-sized creek, and the thick grass growing on the lowlands would provide ample grazing for the stock. Best of all, the place was only three miles from Uncle John's homestead. Joseph was jubilant. The claim was desirable in every way; they would go to Parker the first thing in the morning!

Joseph was in good spirits when they set out for the county seat early the following day. It is true he had some misgivings. What if someone had already filed on that particular claim? He voiced his thoughts aloud. But Uncle was calm and undisturbed. "I wouldn't worry about it, Joe." He had recently fallen into the habit of calling the younger man Joe. Urging the horses on, he continued, "Don't you feel God has led you here?" When Joseph nodded, Uncle went on, "If He wants you to have this place, it will be waiting for you." He spoke so confidently, and with such assurance that Joseph felt his spirits rising. Uncle was right—he would put the matter in God's hands and worry no more about it.

The land office, a small unpainted frame

building, wore a deserted air as the two men walked in the open door. It was quite different in the spring; then the place was crowded with men rushing in to file for their claim. This morning the place was empty except for the clerk sitting at the battered old desk reading an old newspaper.

"Well, what can I do for you today?" he asked, motioning for them to be seated. He was a tall, thin man with a large, prominent nose. His sandy-colored mustache curled slightly at both ends and was stained with tobacco juice, but his blue eyes twinkled, and he seemed to be a good-natured sort of fellow.

He settled back in his chair, pulled his knife from his pocket, and proceeded to sharpen his pencil.

Joseph presented his claim as best he could in his broken, halting English. When he was at a loss for a word, Uncle John helped him out. The clerk asked numerous questions concerning the land site and other information required by the government. Then he unfolded a map, spread it out on the desk, and located the claim, tracing the spot with his pencil.

"Well, there hasn't been any filing done on this particular piece of land, though I must say I can't see why. If it is as good as it appears to be, you are mighty fortunate no one has beat you to it." He hummed a little tune under his breath. Then he leaned back in his chair again, his thin shoulders slightly hunched forward.

"I'm powerful glad to see you get it though; I've heard some good reports about your people," he added, looking admirably at Joseph's stalwart figure. Leaning forward again, he reached into the scarred desk and drew out some papers and a bottle of ink. He filled a pen and began to write. When he had completed the document according to legal procedures, he handed the pen to Joseph. "Just sign your name here, and that will be all that's necessary."

Joseph wrote his signature with a hand that trembled. This was a momentous step in his life. If they succeeded in holding the claim for five years, the land would be theirs. It seemed too good to be true. Uncle was right; God had certainly overruled in the matter. Even the clerk had been surprised the claim hadn't been filed on before now. There was no question in his mind—God was leading them in their choice.

Riding home from Parker, the two men were discussing some of their experiences since coming to America. Joseph wondered if he would ever be able to master the English language.

"If only I could speak and understand English better," he said wistfully as they jogged along the prairie road in the wagon. "It is embarrassing to stutter around and know how funny it must sound to other people," he added ruefully.

Uncle John laughed knowingly. Joe needed cheering up on that score, he decided. "Ha, let me tell you what happened to me when we first came here. It wasn't funny to me then, but I've had a good many laughs about it since. One of my English neighbors asked me if I would bring his mail along home from town since I was going anyway. I agreed to do so. Going into the little country store, I asked for some Mehl. I tried to explain, 'It is for my neighbor, Mr. Campbell, but he didn't give me any money to pay for it.' I spoke in a puzzled voice. The storekeeper scratched the top of his bald head, thought for a moment, then suddenly burst into hearty laughter. 'Ho, ho!' his voice rang out. 'What he wants is his mail.' I had mistaken the German word Mehl, meaning flour, for the English word Mail."

Joseph joined in with Uncle's hearty laughter. He was sure he wouldn't forget that for a long time.

Soon after the trip to Parker, Joseph purchased his first team of horses and a wagon. Mr. Jenkins, an acquaintance of Uncle John's, had been forced to give up his claim on account of illness and was returning to his former home in the East. When he offered the team and wagon for a reasonable sum, Joseph was quick to accept the offer.

Driving home on the dusty prairie road was a thrilling experience for Joseph. The team was a fine pair of powerfully built bays, big yet gentle and easy to handle. They responded to his lightest touch on the reins, prancing along with their necks arched and their glossy manes flowing in the wind. He could hardly wait to show them to Barbara and the girls. Things seemed to be happening fast now—first, the finding of the claim, today the purchasing of the team and wagon, and tomorrow beginning on the house. The house, like many of their neigbors' homes, would be made of sod. These houses were cool in summer and snug and warm in winter.

The neighbors came to lend their assistance, and it didn't take long for the little sod house to take shape. On the chosen site, squares of sod cut from the prairie were laid one on top of the other with a thick plastering of mud between. The plaster was obtained by driving the horses in a circle on a strip of freshly plowed ground. Around and around the horses went. Now and then water was poured in their path until the mud was of the right consistency. The roof was constructed of thatched prairie grass laid on poles cut from small scrubby trees growing along the banks of the creek. There was but one room, two doors, and several small windows.

It was a happy day when the house was finished and ready to move into.

Those were busy days. Now that Joseph and Barbara were to begin housekeeping again, it was necessary to go to town for supplies.

One beautiful morning in late September, the two drove to Parker. The children were left with Aunt Lizzie. Baby Annie was a good baby and slept most of the time. Mary and Fanny spent the day happily running errands for Aunt Lizzie and helping with the dishes. When the chip box was empty, they were allowed to gather more chips as long as they didn't go out of Aunt Lizzie's sight. She had told them of the danger of being lost on the prairie, and they were careful to obey. When the baby was ready for another nap, they took turns rocking her gently in the cradle.

Meanwhile, in town their parents were making purchases. Some cooking utensils, a cast iron cook stove, several pieces of stovepipe, a washtub, and two kerosene lamps completed their furnishings. Food staples came next. Dry beans, potatoes, a barrel of flour, sugar, salt pork, coffee, and tea were the main items on their list. When they added some kerosene and Joseph found a gun that suited him, they were ready to start home. Wild geese were plentiful, and there were rabbits and other small game on the prairie. Joseph hoped to provide meat for the family, and he loved to hunt.

It was late when they reached Uncle John's. Moving would have to be postponed until tomorrow. Over Aunt Lizzie's good supper of cornmeal mush, milk, and fresh homemade bread, the two families shared the day's experiences together. Life had been pleasant in the home of the older couple, and they would all miss these happy times of comradeship. But since the new home was not far away, they could visit when they chose.

By mid-afternoon the next day the young family was nicely settled in their new home. Barbara put the last dish away in the cupboard made of empty store boxes. Everything was in place, and she and Aunt Lizzie looked around the room admiringly. The table and two small benches were homemade. Someone had given Barbara a rocker. Joseph had made the bedsteads too, and on the crude frames they had placed straw ticks filled with fresh, clean straw from Uncle John's new stack. Spread with bright patchwork quilts, generous gifts from Aunt Lizzie, the beds looked comfortable and inviting. At one end of the room stood the stove, and in the corner nearby hung cupboards made of boxes nailed to the wall. Along the west wall by the window stood the table covered with a real linen cloth which Barbara had woven in Russia. The big trunk fitted between the two beds at the south end, and baby Annie's cradle found its place at the foot of the larger bed.

Aunt Lizzie turned to Barbara. "My, it looks nice and homey, doesn't it?" she asked, placing an arm affectionately around the younger woman. "Ach, we are going to miss you so, but I'm glad that you can be in your own home."

Barbara nodded. Her heart was full of happiness, and tears of joy filled her dark eyes. Kind Aunt Lizzie understood and expected no reply.

Supper was over. Mary and Fanny, tired out from the excitement of moving, were fast asleep in their bed. Baby Annie was dozing sweetly in her cradle.

Stepping softly to the bedside of the two little girls, Barbara drew up the bright quilt and tucked it more closely about them. The warm September day had suddenly grown chilly. She moved her rocker in front of the window and sat down to rest. Rocking gently, she watched the beauty of the evening unfold upon the prairie. The twilight hour had always been her favorite hour in the day. She sighed and smiled. She was satisfied, and her cup of happiness was full. God had been so good to them. What did it matter if the little house was made of sod or if the furniture was crude? She felt rich. It is doubtful if any queen was happier in her palace than Barbara was that night.

Joseph came in with a pail of fresh water and set it down on the bench by the door. They planned to dig a well near the house, but until then they would carry their water from the creek.

Joseph crossed the room and smiled down at his wife. "Happy? Do you like our new home?" he asked softly lest he waken the sleeping children.

Barbara beamed happily. "Oh, Joe, I feel rich. I've been sitting here counting my blessings. Isn't God good to us? Our own home at last! Yes, I'm sure we will be happy here. Look at the sky, Joe; did you ever see anything more beautiful?" Her voice filled with awe as she pointed to the moon that was coming up at the far edge of the prairie.

Together they watched the changing scene in silence. One by one the stars came out dotting the sky with their friendly lights. Suddenly the stillness was broken by the sweet song of the mocking bird. Far off in the distance they heard the howling of a coyote. The moon rose higher and shed its silver radiance over the little sod house on the prairie.

# CHAPTER

# 12

October was drawing to a close. The bright golden autumn days had been unusually warm and sunny. Mary and Fanny played happily outdoors and were growing healthy and strong. The parents noted with satisfaction that Mary's thin, pale cheeks were growing rosy and round. Naturally of a slender build, her form had taken on a plumpness that enhanced her frail beauty. She reminded her mother of a bright prairie flower blossoming in the sunshine. Fanny, too, glowed with health and seemed to have an unlimited amount of energy as she romped about on the prairie. Baby Annie, a sweet-dispositioned little one, was also growing and developing normally. These blessings and many more caused the young parents to rejoice and to thank God for the way He had blessed them.

Winter was approaching. Joseph began building a barn so the horses would have shelter during the cold weather. The newcomers had been warned that the winters in Dakota were often long and severe.

With the help of neighbors, it didn't take long to erect the small barn. It was made of rough lumber Joseph had hauled from Parker. As was customary in Russia, the barn and house were built close together. A small shed between joined the two buildings. This was a good arrangement in cold, stormy weather, for the farmer could take care of his stock without going directly out into the storm.

Joseph was thankful for the good supply of hay he had made from the tall, thick prairie grass which grew in abundance on their quarter section. He cut and hauled several loads of wood made from the stunted cottonwoods and wild plum trees growing along the banks of the creek. Wood was scarce in this country; consequently the settlers were obliged to use whatever they could for fuel when their wood supply gave out. A few herds of buffalo still roamed the prairie, and buffalo chips were often used for fuel by the early settlers.

Barbara was a good housewife, and her busy hands were seldom idle. There was the family washing which must be done by hand. This task involved carrying in countless pails of water to be heated on the stove. There were the ironing and mending, the daily cooking and baking, besides many other tasks the pioneer woman must do. She kept the little sod house clean and neat, sweeping the earthen floor with her broom of prairie grass. She washed and rubbed the windows until they sparkled, then with skillful fingers fashioned curtains from an old worn linen sheet. Hemmed with tiny, even stitches, starched lightly and pressed with the old flat iron, these were hung next to the clear glass panes. The simple curtains added a homey touch to the room, and Barbara felt amply rewarded for her efforts. All her life she had never had more than the bare necessities, but from the time she had begun housekeeping, she had somehow managed to make home cheerful and inviting for those she loved.

Sunday was a day looked forward to by the Mennonite settlers. They had erected a simple frame structure for their meeting-house. After their worship services, they usually shared their noon meal, spending the rest of the day visiting together. The opportunity of social contact enriched their lives and offered them a great deal of pleasure.

November came with chill winds. One morning a heavy frost covered the ground. Joseph took his gun and started across the prairie. He hoped he would be able to shoot a goose or perhaps a rabbit for their supper. Some fresh meat would be welcome for a change. He had been so busy he hadn't found time for hunting until now.

The early morning sun was beginning to take away the sting of the sharp, cold air, and Joseph experienced a sense of exhilaration as he walked rapidly along. He already loved this prairie country and felt at home in its wide open spaces. Here the sky was wide and limitless, spreading like an enormous canopy over the prairie, and there was something fascinating about the stillness over the land.

He decided to follow the creek; just yesterday he had seen a flock of geese light there. He was looking too for signs of good trapping grounds. He was sure there were muskrats and other small game along the creek banks. If he were successful, he would be able to supplement their meager income in this way.

In spite of Joseph's enjoyment of the beauty of the morning, there was something that weighed heavily on his mind. Picking his way carefully through the tall grass, he thought of the fear he had kept to himself for months. His troubled thoughts went back to the time in Ohio when he had first begun to notice that there was something wrong with his eyesight. It was as if a veil were blurring his vision. Although both eyes were affected, the right one bothered him more. Barbara had insisted he needed glasses, but after wearing them for nearly a year, there was no improvement, and the condition was growing slowly but steadily worse. He was beginning to be alarmed. Several generations of poor eyesight, and in some cases total blindness, had been in the history of the Schrag family. Naturally, this knowledge caused some anxiety to Joseph, but he had hoped and prayed he would be spared from this. He knew he couldn't keep it from Barbara any longer. Why, only last night when he was reading from the Bible as was his usual custom before retiring, Joseph could hardly see to read the fine print. But it was a familiar Scripture, and he had made his way through somehow, filling in now and then by memory. He knew that Barbara would be upset when he told her his fears, but he had put it off too long already. He would tell her tonight, he decided. Somehow his heart felt a little lighter when he made this decision; surely together they could find a solution to his problem.

As Joseph trudged along deeply engrossed in these thoughts, he almost forgot what had brought him out this cold November day. With a start he realized he had not seen a sign of a goose and began to wonder if they had all gone south.

Turning about, he headed towards home feeling rather discouraged when a sudden whirring of wings startled him. Out of the grass a small flock of geese had emerged and were rapidly taking flight in every direction. The air was filled with their excited cries.

Joseph raised his gun, aimed as best he could, and fired. There was a loud explosion, and a few feathers drifted down. He ran forward eagerly and began to search for the goose in the tall grass. To his joy he found he had killed a fine plump one. Picking it up, he shouldered his gun and set out for home.

That night delicious odors crept from the little sod house. Barbara had plucked the feathers from the goose and carefully spread them to dry. She was saving them for a featherbed, and it would take a good many more to fill the tick she had made. The bird was dressed and stuffed, then roasted to a rich, golden brown. How they all enjoyed the good supper!

The night grew colder outside. Drawing the rocker nearer the stove, Barbara sat down to rock baby Annie to sleep. The little girls had gone to bed early and were already in dreamland. Soon the wind began to shriek and howl around the house, and it sounded as if a blizzard would strike before morning.

The lamplight glowed cheerfully in the windows as Joseph hurried in with a last armful of wood. "It's starting to snow," he announced, taking off his gloves. "I had planned to go hunting again tomorrow, but if this keeps up, I'll have to give it up." His face was sober as he took off his coat and cap and hung them beside the door. Then he crossed the room to the stove to warm his reddened hands.

"My, the wind sounds so mournful, and it seems to creep in under the doors and through the windows." Barbara shivered and moved the chair closer to the stove. She tucked the blanket more tightly around baby Annie in her arms. The child grew drowsy and snuggled closer to her mother.

"We can be thankful we have shelter tonight," remarked Joseph, putting more wood in the stove. He drew up a chair beside his wife.

The fire burned energetically and soon the room grew a little warmer.

They sat in silence for awhile listening to the sounds of the storm. The wind rattled the window panes, but the little sod house stood firm as the strong gusts increased their fury.

With her quick intuition, Barbara noticed that

Joseph was troubled. She sensed something was on his mind, but from past experience she refrained from asking questions. He would tell her when he was ready. But she was uneasy as she continued to rock the baby.

Joseph cleared his throat. Barbara looked at him expectantly, waiting for him to speak.

"Dear, there is something I must tell you tonight." He spoke slowly as though groping for the right words. "I've kept putting it off, though surely you have noticed it—I didn't want to worry you—" He hesitated.

Barbara's lips parted. "Oh, Joe, what is it? Tell me about it," she whispered, looking up into his troubled face.

"Don't be frightened," he said quickly, reaching out and touching her arm. "You know my eyes are bad, but of late they have been so much worse. I kept hoping they would get better, but it's no use, and I'm afraid I'm going blind. It might be that if I could see a good doctor he would be able to help me, but we can't afford that now, anyway." His voice died away almost to a whisper.

As he had expected, Barbara was alarmed. "Oh, you must do something, Joe. Surely there will be a way out."

Joe sighed. "I'm beginning to wonder, Barbara, whether it might not be truth rather than just legend about that ancestor of mine."

Barbara looked at him in ignorant surprise.

"Hadn't I ever told you?" he asked. "Back several generations, according to family tradition, one of my forbears is supposed to have been an atheist who defied God and dared Him to strike him blind. The man went blind. And much blindness has shown up among his descendants. Is God visiting his iniquity 'upon the children unto the third and fourth generation of them that hate' Him?''

Barbara shuddered, and picked nervously at the corner of her faded calico apron. "If so, our little blind Jacob suffered from that man's sin. But I'm not questioning God. What He does is well done. And our little Jacob is seeing now." Tears welled up in her eyes. "As for you, isn't there a doctor in Yankton you could consult?"

Joseph got up and stirred the fire. After a moment's silence he spoke gravely. "Yes, there is no doubt a doctor in a town of that size, but as I said, we simply can't afford it now." Seeing the distressed look on his wife's face, he hastened to add, "If only I can get started trapping, that will bring in a little extra money, and perhaps by spring I can go." His voice took on a courageous tone at the thought, and both their faces brightened.

Barbara put little Annie in her cradle and joined Joseph again by the fire. The teakettle on the back of the stove was boiling merrily, and Barbara decided to make some tea. There was something cheering about a cup of hot fragrant tea on a cold night like this.

She handed the steaming cup to Joseph. "Drink this, dear; it will do you good."

She filled a cup for herself, and as they sipped their tea, they talked over their problem again. Hope sprang up in their hearts and somehow the situation looked brighter. Yes, there would be a way—they would commit it all into the hands of their Heavenly Father.

Together they knelt, and assurance and peace came to their troubled hearts.

By morning they awoke to a world covered with a blanket of snow. The wind had died down, and the prairie was strangely calm and still.

The sun came out, but it was bitterly cold when Joseph put on his wraps to go and water the horses. The bright rays glittered on the snow, and the dazzling whiteness was almost blinding. Joseph hurried through his chores, eager to get back into the warm house.

It took a lot of kerosene to keep the lamp burning those long winter evenings. Most of the time they blew out the light and sat in the semi-darkness. The firelight shone through the cracks of the stove lids, and it was pleasant to sit by the fire and talk.

The little girls begged for stories of the old home in Russia which they scarcely remembered. But the story they loved to hear best was the one about the "little red apron."

Sometimes the tears would come to Barbara's eyes when they talked of their native land, and she would be filled with a sudden longing to see her old home again.

Barbara had carefully saved the drippings from the fat salt pork and other grease. With these drippings she made soap. She made candles too, and these were a great help in conserving the supply of kerosene. As winter wore on, the lamps were used more sparingly.

When the weather permitted, Joseph looked after his trapline. He caught muskrats, foxes and other small fur-bearing animals. Every cent that could be spared was put away to meet the expenses of the anticipated trip to Yankton.

It was early in March before Joseph was able to make the journey, a distance of about thirty-five miles.

After a thorough examination, the physician informed Joseph that he had cataracts on both eyes. This condition, he said, would require the services of a skilled surgeon to perform the delicate operation. He referred Joseph to a doctor in Buffalo, New York.

Joseph's heart sank. How could he possibly afford the trip east and an operation besides? The thought was staggering. Perhaps when the crops were harvested in the fall it might be possible, but that would be a long time to wait.

# CHAPTER

# 13

Spring came. Joseph sold the furs he had collected from his winter's trapping. He made a trip to town and came home with a plow and some seed wheat. Then he set to work to break up the prairie sod. It was hard work following the horses over the rough ground. His hands gripped the plow handles, guiding it the best he could. The tough sod turned up by the sharp ploughshares formed long furrows until there were acres of broken turf drying in the March wind. When the ground was ready, the wheat was planted, and they hoped and prayed for a good harvest.

Summer followed, and the grain looked promising. But one could never tell. Older settlers had experienced disappointments in former years when destruction came in the form of grasshoppers and droughts.

The hot weather hastened the ripening of the Schrags' waving fields of grain, and soon harvest was upon them. God answered their prayers and their first crop yielded surprisingly well.

After the grain was sold, Joseph began making plans for the trip east. By this time his eyesight had grown steadily worse. Barbara and the girls had taken over most of the work, and kind neighbors helped whenever possible.

It was a bright day in early October when Joseph boarded the train that was to take him to New York. Barbara could hardly bear the thought of his traveling alone, but there was no other way.

When his fellow passengers noticed his predicament, they were kind and understanding, lending their assistance whenever possible. The tall, nearly blind man in his thirties had aroused their interest and commanded their respect from the very beginning.

With such pleasant traveling companions, Joseph began to enjoy the trip. He was thankful he had made progress in learning the English language, and although his speech was broken and halting, he got along very well. He had a pleasant surprise at the end of his journey when he was ushered into the presence of the famous surgeon. That man was German too!

After undergoing a thorough examination, Joseph was scheduled for surgery the following day.

The cataracts were removed, and Joseph remained under the doctor's care for some time.

Those were long, tedious days, but the time came at last when the doctor told him the operation had been successful and soon he could enjoy normal eyesight again. Joseph was thrilled. Now he would be able to take his place as before and assume the responsibilities that were his.

When he boarded the train for Dakota that would take him to his loved ones, Joseph was careful to follow the doctor's instructions, and instead of feasting his eyes on the changing scenery, he was content to relax and let his eyes rest. No eye strain for him. He would do his best to obey the doctor's orders.

Home at last! Needless to say there was rejoicing in the little sod house when Joseph was at home with his family again. There were tears of joy when they learned the trip east had not been in vain. Barbara felt as if a great burden had suddenly lifted and rolled away. There had been many discouraging times for the young pioneer mother while Joseph had been away, but these were all forgotten now that he was at home again.

That winter Lizzie was born. Aunt Lizzie came and took care of Barbara and the new little namesake.

The young parents were happy. Life looked brighter and the future more promising than it had for some time. The baby was doing well, Barbara was rapidly regaining her strength, and Joseph's eyes were nearly normal again. They thanked the Giver of all these blessings daily, and their faith was renewed and strengthened.

But life is made up of both joys and sorrows, and the next year brought more trials and discouragements to those pioneering in Dakota. A severe drought followed by a dust storm completely wiped out their promising crops. With true pioneer courage they did not give up, and the following year they patiently tried again. Once more destruction came, this time in the form of grasshoppers. They greedily devoured every bit of green vegetation, leaving the whole prairie brown and barren. After two successive years of crop failure, the Schrags along with the others had to struggle to make a living. In spite of it all, they took heart again, hoping the next year would be better.

By this time Joseph had managed to acquire a cow and some chickens. These provided food for the family, and sometimes extra eggs and butter that were traded for other provisions in town.

Joseph made some improvements, adding a lean-to on one end of the house and whitewashing the walls of the one large room. This made the room light and pleasant. The cookstove did not provide adequate heat, so they solved this problem by making a stove of brick, such as they had used in Russia. The big stove was located in the center of the room, and besides providing additional warmth, it was used on baking days. When the bread was ready to bake, Barbara raked out the fire, leaving only a few coals. Then she placed the loaves inside and closed the door. The heat from the bricks baked the bread to a lovely golden brown.

Life seemed to be going along quite smoothly when Joseph made a discovery that shattered their dreams once more. With a sinking heart he realized the cataracts were coming back. And the doctor had been so sure they would not trouble him again!

"Well, there's no money now for another operation, should it come to that!" Joseph declared gravely one evening when he and Barbara were discussing the matter together. Repeated crop failure had made it difficult to buy the most necessary things to sustain life. The future did not look very bright under the present circumstances.

Barbara assented soberly. She laid aside her sewing and crossed the room to Joseph. "Yes, Joe, times are hard, I know, but God's promises are still the same. He has promised never to leave us nor forsake us. We'll all work together and surely there will be a way out."

"That's true," agreed Joseph. He sat up straight in his chair, and a look of determination came into his eyes. Resolutely he pushed away the troublesome thoughts that had been bothering him. He picked up the Bible and handed it to his wife. "Here, read something. I know we can find comfort there."

Barbara nodded. Turning to the book of Psalms she read one comforting portion after another. Each Scripture seemed to fit their case. She read on, marvelling at the wealth of promises God had for His children. She closed the book, and without speaking they knelt to pray. Together they found a new peace and calmness.

In September John arrived. True, they had

lost a little son by that name in Russia, but it was not uncommon to have two children by the same name if one had been called away by death.

Barbara was busier than ever caring for the new baby and helping Joseph more as his vision grew increasingly impaired.

But there was no time for Barbara to sit idle, and often she was so weary she felt she could hardly carry on. Added to this was the worry of their financial burdens. Uncle John came over and helped them out occasionally, but most of the time they managed by themselves.

They struggled through the long winter and were glad when spring came again. Somehow things looked more cheerful after the bleak, cold winter months. Tender green blades of grass sprang up over the prairie, and the birds too rejoiced as they flitted about in the warm sunshine.

Time passed. Summer came. It was especially hot and dry. The sun beat down with such intensity that it seemed as if the whole prairie would be set on fire. Not a breath of air was stirring, and it grew almost unbearably warm and stifling. Even the sod house was like an oven, and in this oppressive atmosphere the children became cross and fretful.

Fanny was not feeling well. For several days she had moped and was unlike her usual active self. The mother attributed the drooping eyes and listless movements of her little daughter to the weather. It was enough to make anyone ill, she reasoned. She became alarmed, however, when Fanny complained of being cold and soon proved it by shaking with a real chill. The anxious mother put her to bed immediately. The chill was followed by a high fever, and the little sufferer moaned and tossed in her distress.

Barbara sat by the bed trying to comfort the sick girl. This was now the fourth day of her illness, and she showed no sign of improvement. The mother tried her best to bring the fever down. She bathed the feverish body and held countless drinks of water to the parched lips, but all was to no avail. The fever rose steadily; delirium seized her, and she cried out incoherently.

Barbara could stand it no longer. "Oh, Joe, don't you think we had better get the doctor to come and see Fanny?" she beseeched, tears of worry filling her dark eyes. "I have done all I can, and she isn't getting any better." She wiped her eyes with the corner of her apron.

Mary stole to her mother's side, her own tears beginning to fall as she tried to comfort her mother.

Joseph bent over the little girl and placed a gentle hand on her hot forehead. Fanny's dark lashes fluttered and her eyes opened, but there was no recognition as she murmured something unintelligible. The father's dim eyes did not discern the vacant staring in Fanny's eyes, but he knew from his touch that a terrible fever burned in her body, and the child was delirious. He stood up tall and straight, and his face was sober.

"I'll go after Dr. Barnes right away. Prince

knows the way to town, and I'll make it all right. Don't worry; I'll be back as soon as possible."

He stooped and kissed Barbara. "Mary, come and help me saddle Prince."

Mary grasped her father's hand, and the two went out.

On the way to town Joseph had to stop several times to let Prince rest. The dry, hot air had that peculiar sultriness that usually precedes a thunder storm. They needed a good shower to clear the atmosphere and cool things off, but Joseph hoped the storm would hold off until he reached shelter. He urged Prince on.

Dark clouds formed, and a flash of lightning streaked across the darkened sky. A deep clap of thunder pealed overhead as Joseph rode up to the doctor's house, dismounted, and made his way carefully to the door.

The door opened, and the doctor's wife greeted Joseph. "Doctor is out now making a call, but I'm expecting him back soon and I'll give him your message. Too bad about your little girl," she added kindly.

While they were talking, great drops of rain began to fall, and soon the rain began to come down almost in torrents. Joseph gladly accepted the invitation to go inside and wait for the storm to pass. It ended almost as quickly as it had begun, and Joseph stepped out into a wonderfully refreshed world.

Mounting his faithful horse, he set out for home, hoping the doctor would soon follow. Prince too was filled with new energy and jogged steadily along until they reached home.

Fanny was no better, and they kept an anxious vigil waiting for the doctor. It was getting dusk when they heard the sound of buggy wheels approaching. Joseph and Mary met him and took care of his horse while the doctor hurried into the house.

Upon examining the sick child, he pronounced her illness a bad case of malaria. He opened his satchel and took out a small vial of medicine. Then he called for a spoon and administered a dose to the sufferer. All through the long night hours the doctor and parents kept close watch, giving medicine at regular intervals.

Dawn broke over the horizon. Fanny lay quite still now, and the kindly, middle-aged physician sat by the bed with her little hand in his. Her pulse was getting weaker, and her face was wan and pale.

"I can't understand this," the doctor said at last. "She doesn't respond to the medicine as I had hoped, and I'm afraid I can do no more for your little girl." He spoke as gently as he could to the sorrowing parents.

Minutes later merry, dark-eyed Fanny slipped away to be with her Maker.

It was hard to understand why God chose to call Fanny home. What a vacancy there would be! But God's grace was sufficient to carry them through this sorrow, and they bowed in humble submission to His will.

Fanny was laid to rest in the cemetery behind the church. That made five graves since the settlement had been founded in this part of Dakota.

# CHAPTER

# 14

Joseph's eyes grew steadily worse. This great handicap caused more difficulty as time went on. They decided he should see Dr. Barrows again in Yankton. Perhaps he could give some advice.

One morning in late, glowing summer, Uncle John and Joseph made the trip to Yankton. As they jogged along the countryside they talked about their early harvest. Already the crops had been gathered in, and though the grain yield had been small, they were thankful for what they had.

As they climbed the steep stairs to the doctor's office in the large brick building, Joseph's heart was heavy. He hoped he hadn't waited too long to see Dr. Barrows, but it couldn't be helped.

The doctor finished his examination. When he spoke, there was concern in his voice. "Mr. Schrag, I'm sorry to say that surgery is the only answer to your problem. The cataracts have come back and will need to be removed. I realize you may question the success of another operation, and it is only natural that you should; however, this time I am going to refer you to a different surgeon—Dr. Whittier of Baltimore, Maryland. He specializes in cases like yours. I would urge you to give him a chance. It is either that or lose your eyesight altogether," he finished kindly, yet with a note of finality.

Joseph took the news bravely although inwardly his thoughts were in a turmoil. Baltimore, Maryland, the doctor had said. That would mean another long trip east, and besides that, more expenses. They couldn't possibly afford that now, but perhaps later God would make it possible to go east for another operation.

On the way home Uncle John tried his best to cheer Joseph. "There'll be a way out of this, Joe; just wait and see. God always takes care of His own. And we'll all pitch in and help out whenever we can." He stole a look at Joseph's solemn face.

Joseph nodded. "Yes, Uncle, you are right as always." He had to smile a little. One couldn't remain gloomy long in the presence of Uncle John.

Joseph and his family had lived on the claim they had taken as a homestead the required five years. It had been a hard struggle through the lean years to make ends meet. But in spite of financial setbacks, they had succeeded in holding the claim. They had realized the fulfillment of the dream of owning their own home. Now they were faced with one of the hardest decisions of their lives. They were considering selling the homestead so they could meet the expenses of Joseph's much-needed operation.

Hearing of land available for homesteading several miles away, they sold their place and moved to the new claim.

The new homestead was three miles from town. Here they camped temporarily in a small dugout until a house could be built. Little did they realize that nearly two years would pass before Joseph would be able to go east for the operation he so badly needed.

They made plans for the new home. Joseph hauled lumber from town, and work was begun. With his poor eyesight he couldn't drive a nail, but there were some things he could do, and he helped all he could. Uncle John went ahead with the building, and with the aid of the neighbors the frame house was soon finished. Although built of rough lumber, it was larger and more roomy than the sod house. They moved in and were nicely settled before the cold weather set in. Soon afterward a small barn was built, this time some distance away from the house.

In October the mild weather ceased. The cold winds blew through the dried grasses on the prairie and rustled the leaves of the cottonwoods. The older settlers predicted an unusually hard winter.

The hay was cut and stacked, but there was wood to cut and haul. Sometimes one of Barbara's older brothers came to help them with their work. Her parents, the Peter Grabers, had moved to Dakota the year before, but their claim was several miles away, and they weren't able to come over every day. It was up to Barbara and Mary to help Joseph most of the time.

The summer had been so warm and sunny that it was hard to believe winter was near. Then the nights grew colder, and soon one hard frost after another chilled the countryside.

With the coming of cold weather and the predictions of a hard, long winter, Joseph felt they should go to town for supplies. They had lived in Dakota long enough to learn that oftentimes it was almost impossible to go to town during the severe winter months.

Early the following morning Barbara helped Joseph hitch the team to the wagon. There was nothing unusual to indicate a change in the weather as they drove to Marion Junction.

Mary was left in charge of the younger children. It was not the first time the ten-year-old had been entrusted with this responsibility. Secretly, however, she was always a little frightened at the thought, but Papa and Mama had thought her capable, and she resolved to do her best. The morning passed by uneventfully, and almost before she knew it, the clock struck half past eleven. She put more wood into the stove and started to get dinner.

The parents hurriedly finished making their purchases in town. A few hours had made a big difference in the atmosphere. It was growing colder, and there was a suspicious moisture in the air that indicated the possibility of snow. They were glad they hadn't put off the trip to town. A day later might have been too late. Now they were anxious about getting back home. Joseph urged the horses on. The animals seemed to understand the need to hurry and quickened their pace.

Soon they were in sight of home. Smoke curled from the chimney and drifted down. "Father always said that is a sign of rain or snow," Barbara remarked as the wagon came to a stop in front of their house. She had fallen into the habit of describing things to Joseph of late. "And there are the children watching for us at the window." She waved her hand to them. They waved happily back, happy because Papa and Mama were home again.

When the wagon was unloaded and dinner eaten, Barbara helped Mary wash the dishes. Outside, the sky was darkening and the wind was rising.

They did the chores earlier than usual that evening. Together Joseph and Barbara fed and watered the stock. They hurried into the house with the milk just as it began to snow.

Barbara was thoroughly chilled—first, during the ride home from town and then while they were doing the chores. She felt as if she would never be able to get warm again. She handed the milk to Mary, then took off her wraps and rubbed her cold hands. The little ones crowded around, wanting her attention.

Mary strained the milk and placed it on the pantry shelf. She finished setting the table and dished the food. She was such a help and comfort to Barbara and seemed more mature than many ten-year-old girls. Barbara praised her eldest daughter. Her loving words brought a slight flush to Mary's cheeks and made her blue eyes shine.

Barbara slipped into the bedroom and came back with a small parcel wrapped in brown paper. She handed it to Mary. "Here is a little present we brought from town."

Mary's eager fingers reached for it. "Oh, thank you, Mama," she exclaimed happily. With trembling fingers she unwrapped the slim package. The paper fell off and revealed several long sticks of striped red and white peppermint candy. "I'll share it with Annie and Lizzie and little Johnnie too," she added generously.

While they were eating supper the wind blew harder, making strange, mournful sounds. It crept in under the doors. Barbara rolled up a rug and put it in front of the door in an effort to keep out the cold.

That was the beginning of the first of the many blizzards during the winter of 1880-1881. All winter long, for seven months, one blizzard followed another. Not once in all that time were they able to take the horses to town. Sometimes when the weather would be clear for a few days, Barbara's brother Pete would come over on his snowshoes, and he and Joseph would go to town for supplies.

The snow kept piling up and drifting until the house was almost covered. Joseph tried to keep the snow cleared away from the windows and the doors.

One day when it had stopped snowing and the sun was shining, they heard a noise and a shout coming from above them. They stared in amazement when they saw a pair of long legs sliding down in front of the window. A moment later Pete stuck his head in the door.

"Where did you come from, Uncle Pete?" asked little Johnnie. Surprise was written all over his chubby little face.

"I slid right down over the top of your house," Uncle Pete said, grinning. His eyes twinkled merrily. "I wasn't sure where your house was in all this snow, but I found it all right." He picked up Johnnie and swung him high.

Johnnie laughed and shouted in delight. He adored Uncle Pete.

That was the longest winter they had ever endured. Looking back in later years, they wondered how they had survived. They ran out of wood and were obliged to burn twisted sticks of prairie hay to keep warm. Other settlers had the same experience, and they all longed for spring to come.

The month of May brought the long winter to an end. The last trace of snow melted in the warm spring sunshine. Soon the grass sprang up, tender and green. The birds came back, and the air was filled with their sweet songs. It was time to plow and get ready for the spring planting of grain.

A small strip of sod was broken for a garden. The seeds sprouted quickly in the moist earth and made rapid growth.

The entire family needed shoes and clothing. Barbara's ingenuity was taxed as clothes were mended and patched until there was hardly a spot left that had not been repaired. And there were always flour and other staples to buy.

Joseph's affliction was worsening, and with hard times there was no chance of going east. If they would have allowed their minds to dwell on their circumstances, they might have given up in despair. But instead they kept busy, and found work a good antidote for worry.

Cold November arrived. Little Johnnie became suddenly ill with membranous croup. Joseph had gone to town early that morning with a neighbor. The younger children were still asleep when he left, and it wasn't until Johnnie awakened that Barbara discovered his rasping cough.

A strange fear gripped her heart. Croup could be a treacherous thing, and she watched her little son anxiously, wishing all the while for Joseph's return.

She made a tent from an old sheet and steamed him to ease his breathing, but he grew worse in spite of all the remedies she tried.

Later in the afternoon Johnnie complained that his throat hurt. His mother took him in her arms and held him, crooning and trying to soothe him. His face was flushed, and his breath was coming in quick, short gasps. She had never known croup to be so severe in a child his age. Would Joseph never come? She breathed a prayer for help.

Mary brought in the eggs she had gathered. "Mama, Papa is coming now. See, there is Chris Graber's wagon and team coming in the lane." She pointed out the window.

"Oh, I'm so glad." Barbara's voice almost broke in relief. "See, Johnnie, Papa is coming." She moved him closer to the window.

Johnnie's eyes brightened somewhat at the sight of his father.

Joseph was much concerned to find his little son ill. "Let me hold him awhile, Mama; you must be tired." He took his little son in his strong arms and sat down in the chair Mary brought quickly for him.

Johnnie lay back contentedly for a time but soon became restless again.

"Would you rather lie down or shall Papa hold you?" his father asked tenderly.

"Hold me, please, Papa," he answered with difficulty.

"Don't talk if it hurts you, Sonny; just lie back and rest." It hurt Joseph to see his little son suffering. He would gladly bear the pain if he could. Unless the boy was better by morning, they would have to go after the doctor.

They sat quietly for some time. Johnnie lay with his eyes closed. They noticed with alarm that his breathing was becoming more labored. Suddenly he opened his eyes wide and struggled to sit up.

"Papa—" he gasped for breath and choked. He beat the air with his small fists. Then the terrible struggle was over. He would suffer no longer. God had taken their only son unto

Himself.

Hot tears trickled down the faces of the bereaved family. Life is filled with sorrows and heartaches; yet many times these trials prepare us for greater trials ahead. Joseph and Barbara were unconsciously developing traits of courage and fortitude, and although they were unaware of it, God was preparing them for still greater trials in the years ahead.

# CHAPTER

# 15

The Dakota prairie was beginning to show signs of spring. After the cold winds and snow of winter, the warm sun had melted away every trace of snow, and soon the bare earth was carpeted with green grass. The calls of wild geese and other birds filled the air. They were happy too that spring was here with its warm, sunny days and gentle breezes.

Joseph and his young brother-in-law Joe Graber were on their way east to Baltimore. By this time Joseph was almost totally blind, and it was necessary for someone to accompany him on the long trip. Oh, how they hoped the trip would not be in vain. Joseph felt so useless and helpless in his present condition. He knew too that Barbara's strength had been severely taxed many times, but she had never once complained.

"Dear God, please watch over my dear ones at home," he prayed silently as the train sped on its way.

The monotony of the journey was reduced by Joe's picturesque description of the everchanging landscape. The boy described the passengers too, going into detail and painting such vivid word pictures that Joseph felt he knew each fellow passenger by the time they reached their destination. What a comfort young Joe was! In his jolly companionship Joseph's mind was drawn away from his worries, and he felt quite confident when at last they located the office of the famed eye specialist, Dr. Whittier.

Once more Joseph submitted to a thorough examination. Again he was advised to have the cataracts removed. Before they left the office, the physician had Joseph scheduled for surgery within a short time. The sooner the better, was the doctor's advice, and Joseph readily agreed, for that meant the sooner he would be ready to go home.

While Joseph was recovering from the operation, the doctor came in every day to see his patient. One day he announced, "Well, Mr. Schrag, you are doing fine, and I can see no reason why you shouldn't be able to go home soon."

Joseph's heart leaped for joy at the words. "I'm glad to hear that," he replied happily. "We are a long way from home, you know."

"Oh, yes, you live in the Dakota territory, isn't that right?" the doctor asked, leaning back comfortably in his chair.

Joseph nodded.

Dr. Whittier stroked his graying beard meditatively. "Mr. Schrag, is it true there are frequent dust storms and a good deal of wind in that area?"

"Yes, that is right. We have had plenty of both since we have lived out there, but it's a great country in spite of that," Joseph told him, listening closely for what was coming next.

The doctor spoke again, carefully choosing his words. "I am going to advise you to change climates. The wind and dust can be very injurious to those eyes of yours, and you must avoid anything that would cause irritation. Eyes, as you know, are too precious to run any risks." He paused, watching for his patient's reaction.

Joseph sat quietly, listening tensely.

The doctor went on. "I realize this is rather sudden news for you, but again I would say, you must go where you will not be bothered by these conditions. Think the matter over and follow my advice." He rose from his chair. "I must be getting on my way now; I'll see you again tomorrow." He gripped Joseph's big hand heartily.

From the first the physician was attracted to the tall, broad-shouldered, husky young man who had come to him for help. There was something pathetic at the sight of such a noble specimen of manhood having to be led about by the younger man who accompanied him. In the course of their conversation he learned they were Mennonites, and he was interested in knowing more of their belief. His respect

127

deepened when he heard the brief story of their history. Here were a people who had been willing to leave their homeland so they might worship as they chose. The busy doctor hoped to learn more of them.

On the way home Joseph thought a good deal on the doctor's advice. He recalled the doctor's last words when the two bade each other goodby. "Take good care of those eyes, Mr. Schrag, and I'm confident they won't bother you again," he declared emphatically. "And don't forget to follow my advice about changing climates. That is extremely important!" Joseph detected genuine concern in the doctor's voice as they shook hands in parting.

Now as the train rolled on its way, Joseph settled down to do some serious thinking. The doctor's parting admonition still rang in his ears. He and Joe discussed the matter at great length. They both had to admit there were many drawbacks in Dakota. While they liked the country and felt at home, they knew there had been many discouraging times the past few years. The successive crop failures, inevitable grasshoppers, dust storms, and droughts were unpredictable; they could never tell when one or the other would strike. But where could they go? The question remained unanswered for the present.

\* \* \* \* \* \* \* \* \*

Meanwhile at home Barbara was having difficult days. Lizzie, the youngest of the three girls, came down with the measles. She was quite ill for several days, and then when she began to improve, she was cross and fretful. Before she had fully recovered, Mary and Annie became sick with the disease the same day.

Barbara had her hands full. Besides taking care of the sick, there were chores to do, and she herself tired easily these days.

When Aunt Lizzie heard of their plight, she bundled some clothes together, and Uncle John brought her over to stay awhile.

It was a relief to have cheerful, efficient Aunt Lizzie there. She bustled about and began taking charge of things right away. Barbara was told to lie down and rest. She had been kept awake a good deal since the girls had become ill, and her face was pale and drawn. Aunt Lizzie's keen eyes detected this at once, and turning back the quilt, she coaxed the tired mother to go to bed.

She would lie down for only a little while, Barbara told herself, sinking down gratefully. How good it was to rest and leave everything in Aunt Lizzie's capable hands! Her great weariness soon overcame her, and in spite of herself, she drifted off into the first sound sleep for weeks.

Aunt Lizzie tiptoed softly about stirring up the fire, giving drinks to the feverish girls—in short, doing whatever needed to be done. And the exhausted mother slept on.

Uncle John split a big supply of wood and filled the wood box. Then he left after promising to send one of the neighbor boys over to do the chores. Joseph's new homestead was about six miles from Uncle John's.

That night, the eighteenth of March, baby Carrie was born. She had dark eyes and hair like her mother's. Later the family began calling her Carolina Rose because there were other Carrie Schrags. Then that name was shortened to Carrie R. and eventually to Carrie again. Little Carrie's arrival was sooner than they expected, and they knew Joseph would be surprised to find a new little daughter awaiting him when he returned home.

The girls recovered from the measles, and Barbara was soon up and around with Aunt Lizzie's careful nursing. Now as the time drew near for Joseph's return, they all looked forward to his coming. Would Papa be able to see, and would he be able to see baby Carrie? the little girls wondered. That question was on Barbara's mind too. Oh, how she hoped and prayed the operation would be successful this time.

\* \* \* \* \* \* \* \* \*

The train neared Yankton, and soon the jerking motions of the cars indicated they were stopping at the depot. A moment later the call rang out, "Yankton! Get ready! Yankton!"

A tall young man was assisted down the steps by an attentive younger man. The older man's eyes were swathed in bandages. Immediately the crowd which had gathered made way for the two men.

Young Joe scanned the group for a familiar face. Ah, there was Father! He steered Joseph towards Peter Graber, who was edging his way through the group.

"Well, well, back again! How are you, Joseph? And you, Joe?" the gray haired man inquired, grasping the hands of each in turn.

Joseph recognized the voice of his father-in-law at once. "Hello, father. It's good to hear your voice again. How are Barbara and the girls?" he asked anxiously.

"The girls had quite a siege with the measles, but they are fine again. They are eager to see their papa. Barbara is fine too." Grandpa's eyes twinkled merrily. He wasn't going to give their secret away if he could help it. "How did the operation turn out? I see you still have your eyes bandaged."

"The doctor says it is a success, but he ordered me to keep them bandaged for awhile. He especially warned me to protect them from the dust and the wind," Joseph told him.

On the ride home they told Father Graber all about it. The older man was concerned. "Of course, the doctor must be right," he readily agreed. "But it will mean something to have to leave your home and all of us," he ended sadly.

Joseph nodded miserably. It seemed they had faced one hard problem after another. He wondered how Barbara, his dear, faithful wife, would take the news.

Home again! How wonderful to be with the dear ones! And what a happy surprise to find a new little daughter there! The girls were disappointed that Papa couldn't see wee baby Carrie, but he consoled them with the thought that before long he could remove the bandages and be able to see her and all of them.

He sat in Barbara's rocker and tenderly held baby Carrie in his arms. They gathered around him, and he told them all about his trip. He pictured the scenery and described the trip he had seen through Joe's eyes. "I don't know what I would have done this time without him," declared Joseph. He related details of his surgery and told them of the kind doctor who had attended him, but he couldn't bear to tell them what the doctor's final advice had been—not yet; his coming had made them so happy.

Another surprise was in store for Joseph. While he had been away, the men from the settlement had brought their teams and implements to the Schrag homestead. With several teams at work, it didn't take long for a large strip of prairie sod to be broken. After the long furrows had been harrowed, the wheat and oats were planted. When Joseph learned of this kindness, his heart was full of gratitude, and a warm feeling for his brethren welled up in his heart. How could they think of leaving home and friends?

Though the days were still warm and sunny, the nights were growing cool, and the fire felt good. Joseph sat near the stove, his hands resting in his lap. It was so good to be at home again. The girls chattered as they washed the supper dishes. Mary washed, and Annie wiped, while little Lizzie tried to help by putting some of the dishes away. Barbara was sitting by the table with her mending. She was putting a patch on one of Mary's faded dresses. Baby Carrie was asleep in the cradle.

Now and then Barbara glanced at her husband. He had been very quiet since supper, and she wondered uneasily if something was troubling him. But no doubt he was tired from his long journey, and he was content to just sit and relax. She laid down her sewing and rose to put more wood on the fire.

After the dishes were finished, Barbara gently reminded the girls it was time for bed, and they obeyed after kissing their parents goodnight.

The mother picked up her mending again and began stitching where she had left off. The dress wouldn't stand another patching, but maybe she could make it do for a little while longer.

Joseph leaned forward in his chair. He cleared his throat. "Barbara, I hate to tell you this, but you might as well know it now—Dr. Whittier thinks it best for us to leave Dakota." He tried to speak cheerfully for her sake.

Barbara's work dropped in her lap. She sat with clasped hands and waited tensely for his next words. "Go on, Joe," she pleaded. "Why must we leave here? Tell me quickly!"

"Don't be so alarmed, dear; come sit here beside me, and I'll tell you all about it," he said gently.

She crossed the room and drew up a chair by his side. She slipped a hand in his. Then Joseph told her all about it—of the doctor's advice concerning a change of climate and of the grave danger that threatened his eyes if they remained here. He finished by saying, "And now the question is—where shall we go?"

Barbara sat with bowed head. The clock ticked steadily on, and the lamp glowed cheerily casting soft shadows about the room.

Then her head lifted. She spoke to Joseph through a mist of tears. "God has never failed us once, Joe, and He won't fail us now. He provided money for both operations, and when things looked darkest, there was always a way out. After all, your eyesight is the most important thing to be considered, and if that is our only hope, then that is what we must do!" She smiled bravely through her tears.

"That's right," agreed Joseph. "We must leave it all in God's hands. I have been thinking about it almost day and night the past few days, and no doubt we'll have to wait until harvest. In the meantime we must be patient and trust." His voice was hopeful again.

# CHAPTER

# 16

Joseph had been home a week. Morning dawned giving the promise of a beautiful spring day. The weather seemed almost perfect, Barbara thought, as she hung her clothes out to dry.

In the afternoon the breeze that had been soft and warm turned cool, and the sun hid behind a dark cloud that had suddenly appeared in the sky. Soon the blue sky turned to gray, and more clouds darkened it. The wind rose with a mournful sound. It hardly seemed possible that the weather could change so quickly.

In the kitchen Barbara was shaping bread dough into loaves. She glanced anxiously out the window. Here it was the first of April, and it actually began to look as if they were going to have a blizzard! But surely that couldn't be, she told herself, as she finished the last loaf. She covered the bread neatly to rise, washed her hands, and dried them quickly. Then she hurried into the next room.

"It's starting to storm, Joe. You don't suppose we are going to have a blizzard, do you? Listen to that wind!!" Her eyes were filled with worry as a hard gust shook the house. Joseph was alarmed. He sat up straight and erect. "If that is true, we better get the stock in. Oh, if only I were able to go myself!" He spoke almost sharply in his anxiety.

"I'll run out and bring in the clothes first." Barbara put on her wraps. "Mary, be ready to go with me when I come back," she said as she hurried out.

The wind tore at the clothes and almost whipped them out of her hands. At last she managed to get them safely into the house.

Mary was ready, and the mother and daughter hastened out. The animals sensed the approaching storm, and the women had no trouble coaxing them into the barn. They filled the mangers with hay and hurried back into the house. They were not a moment too soon, for suddenly the storm broke in all its fury. The wind shrieked and howled, and the house trembled and shook. Then it began to snow, and the wind whirled it and swished it against the windowpanes in its madness. They were reminded of the long winter two years before.

For two days the blizzard raged. There was not much hay left, and Barbara fed it sparingly. On the morning of the second day she gave the horses and cows the last of it. Now she would have to find her way out to the hay stack some distance away and bring in more. Should she try it? Joseph had warned her to be careful. The storm was not so violent as it had been, but the dim whiteness was almost blinding, and it was impossible to see more than a few feet ahead. But there was no telling how long the storm would last, and the stock would need to be fed. She decided to take the risk and started out.

Barbara could see nothing but the whirling snow. She started in what she thought was the direction of the hay stack. The wind struck her and whipped her skirts around her ankles. It couldn't be much further now, she thought frantically. Another gust brought her to her knees. Struggling to her feet, she plunged on again. She became confused and lost all sense of direction. She would have to give up and go back to the barn, but she was turned around and unknowingly started in the opposite direction.

At the house Joseph and the girls waited anxiously. The minutes seemed hours. The wind was howling and started up with increasing fury. The girls pressed their faces close to the window trying to see if they could catch a glimpse of their mother. But they could see nothing.

Finally Joseph could stand it no longer. Something was wrong. Of that he was sure. He knew it would be foolish to venture out in his condition. His eyes were still bandaged, and even if he removed the bandages he knew the cold wind would be detrimental and perhaps cause serious damage. No, he dared not risk it, but he could call and perhaps she might hear.

He opened the door and called, but his voice was lost in the howling wind. Since there was nothing else he could do, Joseph continued to call at intervals.

*  *  *  *  *  *  *  *  *

Barbara was almost frantic. Where, oh where was the barn? Was she going to be lost on the prairie? Her hands and feet grew numb with cold. She felt she was getting drowsy, and she knew if she didn't find shelter soon she would freeze to death. With one last desperate prayer to God for help, she sobbed and staggered on again.

Then above the tumult and noise of the storm she thought she heard a faint call. She caught her breath and listened, straining her ears. Would she hear it again? Please, God, let me hear it once more, she pleaded silently. It came again, clearer this time. With renewed effort she started on again in the direction from which the sound came. The next thing she knew she had bumped into a wall. What it was she didn't know; she was only too thankful and relieved that she had reached a shelter of some kind. The blow nearly stunned her for a moment, but she roused once more. Feeling her way along the wall, she came to a door just after Joseph had closed it in desperation. Could it be that she was safe at last?

Her cry brought them quickly to the door. They helped her in and took off her frozen wraps. They took off her shoes and tenderly rubbed her half-frozen feet.

Mary brought a cup of hot tea, and Barbara

sipped it gratefully. Slowly she began to grow warm and comfortable. When she felt better she told them how she had tried to go after hay and had lost her way in the blizzard, how she had prayed in desperation and how God had answered her prayer immediately. It was then she had heard Joseph calling, and she had been guided in the right direction and had reached shelter at last.

The mother looked fondly at the little circle of loved ones about her. It was wonderful to be safe in the warm house away from the winds and the cold. Then she thought of the animals without feed in the barn. "Oh, Joseph, the stock must be fed!" she said feebly.

Joseph protested. "Don't worry about them. They won't starve right away, and the blizzard surely won't last much longer. You must not go out there again!" He shuddered to think what might have happened to the one who was so dear to them.

By the next morning the cold wind had stopped blowing, and it was quiet and peaceful on the prairie. The sun came out bright and strong. The blizzard was over, and the stock could be fed again.

# CHAPTER

# 17

Joseph unfolded the letter with trembling hands. For weeks they had been eagerly waiting to hear from Uncle John who had gone to the far western state of Oregon. Would he have a favorable report of the country? Were the glowing stories they had heard of the West true?

Several families besides Joseph's were thinking of migrating. The successive crop failures because of droughts, grasshoppers, and other forms of destruction had been discouraging. Yet this prairie land was home to them, and it was not easy to pull up the roots that had been established. But the unsettled feeling persisted, and it was Joseph's return from the East that had clinched the matter. If there was a place where the climate was more agreeable and farming easier, they were interested in going there. So it wasn't long until their decision was made and Uncle John, their acknowledged leader and advisor, was delegated to make the long journey west. Oregon, the land of promise, was calling. Nearly two months had passed since his departure, and they were eager to hear from him.

When the welcome letter came, Joseph read aloud while the rest listened eagerly. Although his eyesight was much improved by his recent surgery, his vision was not clear, and the condition was not improving as they had hoped. Several times he hesitated and frowned in perplexity as he read the lines penned by his uncle.

"Here in Oregon, crop failures are unknown," he read. "The winters are mild, and there is plenty of rainfall. Besides, there is an abundance of fruit—apples, pears, cherries, peaches, and berries." Joseph paused to explain, "Just think of all that! It sounds wonderful, doesn't it?" He leaned back in his chair, a rapt, faraway look in his eyes.

"Yes, it does sound good, I must admit," answered Barbara, catching some of his enthusiasm. She had to smile at his eagerness. It made him look so much younger. Though Barbara dreaded the prospect of another long journey, she would gladly be reconciled if the move west would improve her husband's eyesight. She was quite sure that her parents would be staying here in Dakota, and the thought was almost unbearable.

The weeks sped by, and harvest time arrived. While the crops were not bountiful, the grain yielded fairly well. The gardens too had produced better than expected in spite of the hot, dry spell in July.

Meanwhile Uncle John had returned, and excitement ran high among the group making plans to go west. There were five families involved in this new venture, and all bore the name Schrag. However, none of them were close relatives of Joseph's.

They were disappointed that Uncle John and Aunt Lizzie would not be going along. Although Uncle John was enthusiastic about Oregon, he and Aunt Lizzie were satisfied to remain where they were. The prairie land was home to them, and they were content to spend their declining years there.

Those who had become land owners sold their property and most of their possessions, keeping only the few belongings that could be taken with them on the train. The Schrags hadn't lived on this claim long enough to prove the homestead. It didn't take long to dispose of their stock, implements and household furnishings, all few in number.

The large trunk that had come all the way from Russia was brought out and packed once more. What to take along and what to leave behind created a problem for Barbara. A few dishes, cooking utensils, the old clock, the family Bible, and some cherished keepsakes were packed in snugly with the clothes. When it was full, she closed the lid declaring there was not room for another thing. Each family planned to take enough food for the entire trip, and Joseph helped her finish packing the box containing their supplies.

The day of departure came. Barbara's father would soon arrive to take them to the train depot at Yankton. She dreaded the thought of the coming separation. Last night they had spent with her parents, and they had bidden good-by to her stepmother, brothers, and sisters. The youngest little sister, Lena, was only twelve days older than their own little dark-eyed Carrie. It was hard to leave her beloved family, but Barbara knew she must brace up for the sake of her own little family.

She looked around the room. Stripped of its furnishings it seemed bare and cheerless. Except for the trunk, box, and a few small bundles, it was empty. Events of the past few years flashed briefly through her mind. Here they had experienced both joys and sorrows; yet God had sustained them through the trying times. She wondered what the future might have in store for them, but she was confident that He would be with them no matter what might come.

Glancing out the window, she caught a glimpse of father's wagon and spirited team coming up the lane. She must not stand idly dreaming. The men would be coming in soon to begin loading.

In the adjoining room baby Carrie, now almost nine months old, had awakened from her nap. She rolled off the old quilt on the floor and began to creep through the doorway into the next room, startling her mother.

Barbara gathered the baby up in her arms in a close embrace. She pressed a kiss on one rosy cheek, murmuring words of endearment. Baby

Carrie was so sweet and precious.

The girls came running in with the news of Grandpa's arrival. Caught up in the excitement about them, they hardly knew whether to be happy or sad. Mary, now a demure maiden of twelve, hadn't forgotten the train ride from Ohio to Dakota. She felt quite experienced and grown-up, while Annie and little Lizzie were eagerly looking forward to the wonderful event.

The big chest was hoisted up on the wagon, followed by the box of food and smaller bundles. The little girls scrambled up to find seats, and Grandpa tucked an old quilt around them. Joseph helped Barbara up to her place on the wagon seat. Baby Carrie came next and was handed up to her mother. The men took their places, one on either side of Barbara, and with a word to the horses, they were off.

It was the first of November in the year 1882, and the air was chilly. The horses stepped briskly, taking the settlers steadily away from the familiar surroundings. Mile after mile across the prairie they traveled. It would take most of the day to reach Yankton where they would board the train that would carry them west.

At the depot they met the rest of their party. Then the rush began. The tickets had to be purchased and their luggage checked. At the last minute there were tearful partings as more than one family bade good-by to their loved ones. Would life always be filled with tears and partings? It seemed so to Barbara as she waved a last good-by to her father from her seat by the window. The train started and before long her father was out of her sight. She choked back the tears and busied herself with the baby.

At this time there were no passenger trains running through the Rocky Mountains to the west coast. Their route would take them indirectly to California. From there the remainder of the trip would be taken by boat along the coast north to Portland.

It was damp and uncomfortable in the poorly-heated train. They made frequent stops along the way, taking on more passengers and picking up freight in the boxcars. They passed through deserts and snow-capped mountains.

After nine long, weary days they entered California. Here the children had their first glimpse of apples. Acres of orchards loaded with fruit of different kinds were an interesting sight to the children who had been born and reared in the Dakotas.

The train stopped at San Francisco where they spent the night in a hotel. The next morning the company boarded a steamboat. From the bay they sailed out into the Pacific.

A voyage of several days brought them to the Columbia River. After leaving this large river, they steamed into the Willamette where they docked a little later at Portland. But they were not yet at the end of their journey. Here they hired a livery wagon to take them to the train depot. Once more they boarded the train, this time for the little town of Hubbard, thirty-five miles south of Portland.

Uncle John had advised them to go to the little settlement of Amish folk near Hubbard. He had told them that they could be sure of a welcome at the Jonas Kauffmans. So it was that the entire group arrived at the Kauffman home. The family lived in a large, two-story, frame house. The sudden arrival of so many unexpected guests seemed to cause no anxiety to their calm, placid hostess. She assured them there would be room for all. And she was right; when the beds were filled, quilts and blankets were laid on the floor for the children, while the men slept in the barn. The hospitality of the Kauffmans was outstanding in the memory of the newcomers long afterwards. Grandma Kauffman, as everyone affectionately called their hostess, proved to be a kind benefactress to many other weary travelers who found their way to her door.

Soon after arriving the emigrants heard that land was cheaper around Dallas, which was about 45 miles southwest from Hubbard. The men soon left to investigate the possibility of settling in that area while their families stayed on at the Kauffman home.

The country south of Dallas was hilly with thick stands of oak and some fir. Small patches had been cleared for cultivation, and while the land was cheap, they learned it was not so fertile as some parts of the Willamette Valley. But the country appealed to them, and since there were several places for rent or sale within an area of a few miles they made their decision. By clearing more land they hoped to be able to raise some crops. Wood could be sold in town, and they felt they could provide a living for their families. Several bought small farms. Others, like Joseph, decided to rent. Joseph rented the Stafford place for one year.

Thus a new settlement was founded about three miles south of Dallas, the county seat of Polk county.

For the first few years the group held church services in their homes. Christ Schrag served as their exhorter until their minister, Jacob Schrag, joined them. Mutually sharing each others' joys and sorrows knit the little band of believers close to one another, and they seemed like one big family. How thankful Joseph and Barbara were that they had all of these dear friends. It made the move to Oregon much easier.

Spring came following a mild winter. After the blizzards in Dakota, it hardly seemed as if they had really had winter here.

Then summer came. Warm days in early June hastened the ripening of the wild strawberries scattered over the hills. Away from the shade and in the open spaces the warm sun shone on the clusters of berries.

One morning Mary, Annie, and four-year-old Lizzie climbed the hill behind the house. They were going berry picking, and each carried a small tin pail. Now and then they stooped to pick a juicy berry along the way. Reaching the top of the hill, they rested awhile, but not long. It was so exciting to see who would find the most berries. They ran here and there searching among the leaves where the berries lay temptingly hidden. Now and then they popped some into their mouths. It was hard to resist the taste of the sweet little fruit, but most of the berries went into their pails, and the girls had hopes of filling them before noon.

Lizzie, however, lagged a little behind the others. Not many berries were in her pail.

"I'm tired picking berries, and I want to go home. I'm hungry and I want a piece of bread," she complained fretfully. Her face was flushed and she sat down on the ground to rest.

"You'll have to wait awhile, Lizzie. We want to fill our pails first. Then we'll go home, and you can have some bread," big sister Mary answered, searching for more berries among the grass.

Lizzie dug a bare toe into the loose dirt. She was tired and hungry and oh, so hot!

"Well, if we don't go now, I won't eat any when we get there, then," she replied crossly. Impatiently she waited for the girls to fill their pails.

At last they were full. Mary had finished filling Lizzie's pail too. She gave it to seven-year-old Annie to carry and took Lizzie's hand. Then the girls started down the hill for home, carefully picking their way through the oak grubs and underbrush.

Lizzie held back and seemed in no hurry to go home.

"What is wrong with you, Lizzie?" Mary was almost out of patience with her little sister. "I thought you were in a hurry to go home so you could have some bread. Come, let's go a little faster," she urged, coaxing the little girl along.

"I told you I won't want any then," Lizzie declared again rather stubbornly.

Mary stared in surprise. This behavior was so unlike Lizzie's usual sunny disposition. When they reached the house at last, their Mother praised them for the nice berries. Unnoticed at first, Lizzie went at once to the homemade lounge and lay down. When her mother saw her there a little later, she soon discovered that she had a very sick child. The little one's cheeks burned with fever, and her eyes were strangely bright. Later on in the day a fine rash covered her body, and her throat was sore and swollen.

The next day Joseph went to town after Dr. Meade. Lizzie was growing worse, and they were much concerned.

Dr. Meade was not long in diagnosing his small patient's illness. "She has a bad case of scarlet fever, and I'm afraid it will take a higher power to get her over this," he said gravely, the words bringing a chill to their hearts. "However, we'll do what we can. I'll give her some medicine that might help to bring the fever down." He administered the liquid between the parched lips. "Give her a dose of this every hour," he instructed, picking up his worn satchel and leaving.

The next day little Lizzie lay very still. Her thin face was wan and peaked. She had eaten nothing since the day she had become ill—not even a piece of bread. But she constantly begged for water to quench her burning thirst. Her parents felt she had reached a crisis and they

149

hovered near, watching for any change.

About noon her eyes opened, and she looked up and smiled feebly. They leaned closer and heard the faint whispered words, "I'm going to be with Jesus." She gave a faint little sigh and was gone.

Aunt Polly and Aunt Fannie came over and prepared the little body for burial. In her pure white dress Lizzie looked almost angelic.

Small Carrie was too young to understand what had taken place. "I want a white dress, too, like Lizzie's," she begged.

The morning breeze was fresh and sweet. Slowly the procession made their way laboriously up the hill over the trail so recently cleared of trees and tangled underbrush. The small homemade casket was borne by four men. When they reached the top they put their burden down by the newly-dug grave. Here, in the level, open space, surrounded by a few firs and small oaks, was the spot they had chosen for their cemetery. Little Lizzie's passing reminded them that death had followed them to this country too, and hers was the first grave on the quiet hilltop.

The sun's rays were warm, but a soft, cool breeze was refreshing after their climb. Now and then the silence was broken by a bird's sweet trill. The men stood with bared heads as the group gathered around the open grave.

The minister spoke briefly, and the words of the short message were of comfort and solace. He spoke of the resurrection day when they would be reunited in the home above and where there would be no more partings. The words brought comfort to their aching hearts. Someday they would see Lizzie and the others who had gone on before.

# CHAPTER

# 18

The following year the Schrags bought a twenty-five acre place. The house was small, with two rooms and a little unfinished room upstairs. Later they added a lean-to which served as their kitchen. The well was handy on the back porch, and they used an oaken bucket to draw their water from its cool depths. The water was good and icy cold.

Like the surrounding country, their place was heavily wooded with oaks. Joseph set to work to clear more land. He felled the trees and dug out the stumps. Soon they had enough wood for their own use and some to sell.

Since coming to Oregon they had not been able to afford a wagon and team. This was a great handicap, and once again they had to depend on their neighbors. Uncle Andrew lent Joseph his team and wagon to haul the wood to town.

Joseph was now wearing glasses with thick,

strong lenses  The time spent in Oregon had brought no improvement to his eyesight. Instead his vision was rapidly fading, and they were faced with the bitter truth—Joseph was going blind. The outlook was dark for a man not yet forty. It hurt him to think he wouldn't be able to assume his responsibility much longer in helping to provide a living for his family. Barbara tried to be cheerful for his sake and made no effort to spare herself. Her former inclination to worry at some fresh new trouble gave way to a new courage and determination. She put her shoulder to the wheel and helped to keep things going.

Although the soil was poor, Barbara managed to raise a fairly good garden. She kept the table supplied with vegetables for her family. She was a good gardener and especially particular about her hoeing. Armed with a good sharp hoe, she hoed deftly around the plants, carefully smoothing the soil as she went skimming down the row. She taught her girls to be good hoers too.

Although they never went hungry, money was scarce and luxuries were unknown. They were forced to skimp and save in order to make a living, but they had been no strangers to poverty.

On October 12, 1884, on a cool Sunday afternoon, identical twin baby girls were born. They were named Fannie and Lillie. Little Carrie's dark eyes filled with wonder and delight when they showed her the babies.

Two babies instead of one meant extra work for the mother. Mary and Annie were good helpers when they weren't in school.

When the twins were only two months old, Barbara was compelled to go to work in town. There were several wealthy families who needed a capable woman to bake their bread and wash and iron their clothes. Already the town people had learned that the sturdy, plainly dressed Mennonite woman knew how to work. Barbara soon found enough work to keep her busy as often as she could get away from home.

On school days she left Carrie and the two babies with Uncle Andrew's family. Aunt Lizzie, a sweet motherly woman, had a little one of her own. Polly was the same age as the twins, a plump, dark-eyed, good-natured baby. Both mothers nursed their babies, and often while Barbara was away all day, Aunt Lizzie nursed all three.

After leaving her little ones, Barbara walked to her work in town. From early morning until late afternoon she washed clothes, cleaned house, and baked bread. It was hard on the young mother who hadn't had time to gain back her strength after the birth of the babies.

Sometimes Joseph accompanied Barbara on these trips. There were people in town who wanted wood cut into stove lengths, and Joseph found that by using a measuring stick of the proper length he could cut wood with his bucksaw. It gave him some satisfaction to think he was not altogether useless.

When evening shadows began to lengthen, Mary and Annie at home watched eagerly for the return of their parents. Many times they could hear the two coming even before they caught sight of them. They could hear their father's deep, rich voice singing in their native German tongue, "What a friend we have in Jesus." Strong and clear, his voice floated through the trees in the gathering twilight. How wonderful it was to have a Friend who knew all about their needs!

Another year passed. Mary was now sixteen. She had not been entirely well after the siege of measles in her childhood. The disease settled in her right leg. From that time on the limb did not develop normally; consequently it was a trifle shorter than her left leg. This abnormality caused her to walk with a slight limp, a condition that was growing noticeably worse. Finally she began to use a cane.

A newer symptom that alarmed her parents now was the nagging cough that began to trouble Mary. This cough was accompanied frequently by flushed cheeks and an unusual brightness in her blue eyes. They heard of a good doctor in Monmouth who they hoped would be able to help Mary, and Uncle Andrew consented to drive her there. The doctor kindly persuaded them to allow Mary to remain in his home for treatment. During the several weeks she stayed there he treated her for tuberculosis, the disease which had fastened itself on her slight body.

It wasn't possible for the family to visit Mary often during her stay at Monmouth since it was about 15 miles from home. On one occasion when they made the trip, the girls were privileged to see their first live bear. The good-sized cub was chained to a pole near the center of the small town where it attracted much attention.

Spring came. Joseph had set out a young peach tree in the fall, and with the arrival of spring, it was putting out leaves and showing signs of growth. Joseph drove four stakes into the ground and by feeling carefully, nailed some boards on these to protect the young tree. The three-year-old twins stood watching close by. Every time their father hit the nail with the hammer they batted their eyes. This experience was amusing to the two little girls and an incident they remembered throughout life.

Now Joseph was almost totally blind. He could distinguish light from darkness, but that possibility too was soon taken from him.

The following winter Joseph became very ill with pneumonia, and it took a long time for him to recover from the illness.

Mary was still ailing, with the troublesome cough persisting. She tired easily and spent much of her time lying on the old couch by the window. She was nearly eighteen, a lovely girl with deep blue eyes and thick blond hair.

The first of May another baby girl, Nellie Mae, was born to the Schrags. As she grew older the twins almost idolized their baby sister. How could they help it when she was so sweet? Blond, blue-eyed, and chubby, she learned to creep and pull herself up to a chair when she was only six months old. Fannie and Lillie spent many happy hours pulling Nellie around in the little homemade wagon Uncle Andrew had made for them.

One day as they were pulling the wagon with Nellie in it along the garden fence by the black raspberry bushes, a large snake glided across their path. The girls screamed, dropped the wagon tongue, and ran to their mother who was hoeing in the garden. Barbara rushed over and killed the snake with one stroke of her hoe. Then she gently reprimanded the girls for leaving Nellie alone in the wagon.

October was bright and sunny. The leaves on the vine maple were turning a brilliant red. Scattered over the hills among the mixed shades of green and gold of other foliage, the colors were a beautiful sight. Down along the winding road that led to town, bright stalks of goldenrod added beauty to the peaceful autumn scene.

Mary lay in her bed by the window. They had moved her bed into the sitting room since she was no longer able to be up and about. Uncle Jake and Aunt Fannie came to see her nearly every day, and she looked forward to these visits.

Dr. Meade came out from Dallas several times to see Mary. He warned them to keep the baby away from her since the disease could be contagious, but they found his orders hard to obey.

"I'm sorry, Mary," mother told her gently, "but doctor said Nellie shouldn't get too close, or she might get sick too."

"That won't matter at all, Mama," the sick girl said matter-of-factly, "because Nellie is coming soon after me." Her eyes were dreamy and bright.

The parents were startled. Why was Mary talking like this? It must be her sickness, they reasoned, yet getting little comfort in the thought.

"Please let me have her here in my arms a little while, Mama," she begged again a little later, and Barbara gave in helplessly.

One evening after the work was done, they were all cozily together in the livingroom. Barbara was busy with her mending. Joseph sat in the rocker by the stove enjoying the warmth of the fire. The twins and Carrie were happily playing with Nellie who sat on a quilt on the floor. Annie sat near Mary with a bit of sewing too in her lap.

The children played quietly. The clock ticked steadily on the shelf on the wall, and the fire crackled and burned with new energy. The nights were growing cooler, and it was pleasant and cozy in the little house.

Mary was very quiet all evening, her watchful mother observed. Suddenly she rose up and startled them all by saying, "I want all of you to listen to me. I have something to tell you." She paused, waiting for their attention.

Immediately they all became quiet. Even baby Nellie seemed to know something unusual was about to take place, and clasping her little hands, she sat still when Mary started to speak again.

"I know now when I am going to die," Mary began, and her voice was perfectly calm. "It was revealed to me that I'm going home at two

158

o'clock. I'm not sure, though, if it will be in the afternoon or early in the morning." She spoke thoughtfully looking at the clock. There was not a trace of worry or fear on her delicate face. "Oh, yes, I saw my crown too," she added dreamily. Then she sank back on her pillow, tired from her exertion.

She lay quietly now and smiled tenderly as her mother came to her side and pressed a kiss on her forehead with quivering lips.

Mary shook her head. "Don't grieve, Mama dear; think how happy I'll be!"

Barbara nodded in agreement but couldn't trust herself to speak.

The next morning Mary lay in a stupor, rousing occasionally as a fit of coughing seized her and then drifting off again. As the day wore on there was little change. She was resting easier now but about an hour later roused again, this time raising her head. She looked out the window.

"Oh, they are coming to meet me!" she exclaimed falling back weakly on her pillow again.

"Who's coming? Is it Uncle Jakes?" Barbara looked out expecting to see them coming as they often did this time of day.

"No, I think it's Grandma." (She had never seen Grandma Schrag.) "And yes, Johnny and Fanny are coming to meet me too. Oh, don't you hear that music?" Smiling she lifted up her hand as if she were shaking hands three times. Her hand dropped to her breast; she gave a little sigh and with a beautiful smile passed peacefully on. The clock on the shelf struck two.

Mary's death was on November 7, and a few days later they buried her on the hill by Lizzie. Joseph carried Nellie in his arms, Barbara guided him along the upward path, and Fannie held on to her mother's other hand. Annie clasped the hands of Lillie and Carrie.

Again they stood around the open grave on the hillside. "Let not your hearts be troubled . . ." The minister spoke the comforting words from John 14.

Charlie Farley, a close neighbor, shaded his eyes with his hat. His manly form shook with sobs. Mary's sunny disposition had endeared her to all who knew her. How they would all miss her! But they knew she was free from all pain and suffering, and they could not wish her back.

Five days later little Nellie became very ill in the night. As the night hours wore on, the baby went into one convulsion after another. Barbara applied home remedies, trying to ease the suffering child, but her efforts were futile. Joseph tried to help, and they took turns holding Nellie.

Just as morning was breaking the baby gave one last shudder and died in her mother's arms.

Annie was sent after Aunt Fanny, who washed and dressed the plump little body tenderly. Barbara brought out a little white dress and handed it to Aunt Fanny. Then she gave way and sobbed uncontrollably.

Aunt Fanny let her cry for awhile. "Go ahead and cry, dear; it will do you good. God knows you've had your share of troubles, but we must

160

not question His will." She put her arms about Barbara and mingled her tears with the bereft mother's.

When the twins got up in the morning and were told Nellie had died, they couldn't believe it; only the day before they had pulled Nellie in the little wagon around the yard. Their darling baby dead! Aunt Fanny drew them gently where they could see the little form lying in front of the window. Tearfully they looked at the sweet little one who appeared as if she were only sleeping. But she was cold and still. In her chubby little hands Aunt Fanny had placed a small bunch of myrtle leaves.

When they took Nellie up to join her sisters in the cemetery, the twins kicked and screamed. "Don't let them put our baby in the hole!" they cried as if their little hearts would break.

They returned to a house that was strangely still. There was no golden-haired baby to creep about the rooms, and Barbara's arms felt so empty. Only yesterday they had been enjoying her sunny smiles and prattling ways. But life must go on, and they dared not grieve in idleness.

The weather had turned colder. Joseph and Barbara hurried home one evening from a hard day's work in town. The month of November was over half gone, and it began to feel as if winter would soon be here. Joseph carried his buck saw and Barbara his dinner pail. She usually ate dinner at the place where she was working.

"I don't know why I feel so chilly tonight,"

Joseph commented, pulling his coat collar up to keep out the cold air. His teeth were almost chattering, Barbara noticed with concern.

By morning Joseph was unable to get up. He had developed a fever, and Barbara feared it was pneumonia again. The next day she sent Uncle Jake for the doctor. When Dr. Meade came, he gravely told her she was right. But he left some medicine, and by careful nursing, Joseph should soon recover, he reassured Barbara.

That night her fears mounted when Joseph told her gently that he wasn't going to get well this time. For several days, he hovered between life and death. The doctor came out again and left more medicine.

One evening their minister Jacob Schrag and his wife called to see Joseph. The fever had gone down, and the sick man seemed to be getting better. Preacher Schrag visited awhile and said he was going over to Uncle Dan's for a few moments. His wife remonstrated with him, urging him to stay, but he left, promising not to be gone long.

Soon after that, Joseph told Barbara he was hungry. Her heart leaped for joy. It was the first time in days he had really wanted food. She hurried to the kitchen to prepare a cup of tea and some toast.

While she was gone Joseph sat up on the edge of the bed. He began to sing, "My heavenly home is bright and fair; Nor pain nor death can enter there," ending with the words, "I'm going home to die no more."

Barbara brought the tea and held the cup to his lips. He took one sip. "Lay me down quick, "I'm dying," he said and began to breathe heavily.

The minister's wife sprang to help Barbara. Gently they laid him down. Annie and Carrie were told to run quickly the quarter of a mile to Uncle Dan's. When they returned with the minister, their father was gone.

Preacher Schrag couldn't believe Joseph was dead. "He seemed to be feeling so much better tonight," he kept saying over and over remorsefully.

It was just dusk, and the minister called for a light. He took Joseph's hand and felt vainly for a pulse. He put his ear to Joseph's heart and listened in vain. Then he called for a mirror to hold to Joseph's mouth. Yes, Joseph had gone to the heavenly home he had been singing about a little while ago. In September he had reached the age of forty, the prime of his manhood. He had still been a stalwart man in spite of his blindness.

While Barbara had many sympathizing friends, no one could realize how deeply she suffered the loss of Joseph. Even if he had been rendered almost helpless at times, it was such a comfort to lean upon him during their bereavements and hard circumstances. Now he was gone, and she had to bear the responsibilities alone. To lose three members of her family within one month's time was a severe trial to her faith. When six-year-old Carrie asked tearfully if they were all going to die, Barbara found herself wondering the same thing. Joseph was buried beside his three daughters. No other graves were added to the little cemetery on the quiet hilltop, but in the last day when the trumpet will sound, we have the assurance that these four will be caught up to meet their Lord.

"How can you be so brave?" her friends often asked Barbara in the days following.

"You can do anything if you have to!" Barbara would reply through trembling lips. "Besides, I have the girls to provide for, and I have to go on. God has promised to be with us, and we are trusting in Him," she would add courageously.

# CHAPTER

# 19

The next summer Barbara and the girls picked enough wild strawberries to pay for Joseph's casket. This was not an easy task. It took many hours of hot, tiresome work climbing the hills near their home to gather the small fruit. Some of the berries were sold to the stores in town. Some found a ready sale among Barbara's employers, who were glad to help the fatherless family in their struggle to make a living.

There were never many moments of idleness. Barbara continued to work for the town folks. Fourteen-year-old Annie, too, found employment, and together mother and daughter walked the three miles to town almost every day. Carrie and the twins were left with Uncle Andrew's. Dear, kind Aunt Lizzie! Barbara often wondered what she would do without her. This aunt had cared for her babies when they were small and was still opening her home and big heart to them.

Sometimes after the evening chores were done and supper was over, they went visiting. They liked to go to their nearest neighbors, the Reasoners, who lived on up the hill beyond them. Barbara always took some mending along so she wouldn't get behind in her work. The girls and young Johnny had jolly times popping corn, playing games, and eating the rosy apples Mr. Reasoner brought from the cellar. These delightful evenings helped Barbara and her family through many hours that would otherwise have been sad and lonely.

Barbara became known among her friends as a woman of unusual courage. Necessity had helped her overcome her fears to a great extent. Now, left without the companionship of a loving husband, she was forced to make all the decisions alone. No, not alone, for her inner strength came from God for whom she was living a life of devotion. She was responsible for the welfare of her children, and she desired above all else to bring them up in the fear of God. She taught them early to love and obey God and His Word.

In spite of her troubles and sorrows, time dealt kindly with Barbara. Her black hair was only faintly tinged with gray. Her form was erect with the right amount of plumpness, and her dark eyes twinkled in her happier moments. But her hands were rough and worn from countless washings and hard work.

Coming home from work one evening in the twilight, Barbara neared the large cemetery south of town. She noticed some movement among the tombstones. It looked like the form of an angel. Could it be? Without further hesitation she climbed over the fence and walked quietly towards the object of her curiosity. As she drew near a large stone, a big owl spread its wings and flew away into the fast-gathering darkness. Barbara smiled a little; she might have known it would be something like that, she told herself, as she went quickly back to the road.

At the supper table she told the girls about it. "And to think it was only an owl," she calmly told them. But they were horrified and wondered how their mother could have been so brave. It is no wonder her children always felt safe and secure when their mother was near.

Not far from their home on the lowland were large fields of fall crops. In late summer when these were being harvested, Barbara and her girls were among the crew of pickers. When finished there, the family moved on to other fields farther away. Here they camped temporarily so they could be near their work.

Many Indians came from the Grand Ronde Reservation each year to work in these same fields. The twins and Carrie were intrigued by the strange dress and dark skins of these people. The little black-eyed papooses strapped on the backs of their mothers working along the rows were especially fascinating. Barbara and Annie had seen an Indian family on the boat as they traveled up from California, but Carrie had been too young to remember the occasion.

The Indians and the whites enjoyed ball

games together, especially on holidays. Their playing was merely recreational, never professional. Sometimes Barbara's girls watched these games. This diversion, along with picking fall crops and other activities, was stamped indelibly on their memories

The little colony of Mennonites grew. Several more families located in the area, and the group became too large to continue meeting in their homes for church services. They felt it was time to build a place of worship and decided to erect a building in the north part of town.

Soon the sound of hammers and saws was heard as the men began to construct the frame building. Finally the house of worship was finished, and the group gathered with thankful hearts for their first worship service in the simple structure.

Their members were a little more widely scattered now. Some came in wagons and buggies, others on horseback, and some walked.

The time came when Barbara felt her family should have their own means of transportation. They purchased a snow-white pony and a single buggy from the minister's son. Sam was a lively fellow who had been trained for race track and high jumping, and had performed at Fourth of July celebrations. It was impossible to keep him in the pasture, so he was kept in the barn, and they had to make sure the door was securely shut and bolted. He was a good riding pony, however, and he pulled the single buggy obediently until they came to a steep grade or hill. There he would come to a halt, and no amount of coaxing would persuade him to move. Finally Annie would get out of the buggy and take hold of his bridle. "Come, Sam," she would plead, and he was always ready to start off obediently again.

Nearly two years passed. Among the newcomers in the community was a widower, David Unger. He had come from Manitoba, Canada, and was a pleasant, congenial man in his early sixties. From the first he had been attracted to Barbara. His children were grown and had homes of their own, and he was lonely and hungry for companionship. Barbara, on the other hand, had never dreamed of marrying again. No one could take Joseph's place in her heart, and when David first made known his interest in her, she was very reserved in her manner towards him. When she didn't encourage his attention, some of her friends chided her and spoke almost unkindly, criticizing her actions. They urged her to reconsider and accept his offer of marriage. "If anyone needs help, you do, and if you don't marry him, don't expect much help from us," they told her pointedly.

Barbara wept and prayed, seeking God's leading in her life as at other times. It had been a hard road to travel alone— how well she knew. Finally she yielded and promised to be his wife.

The wedding was held in the new church. Following the ceremony a reception was given in their honor at the home of the Peter Goerings, who lived nearby.

Barbara's children soon learned to love and respect their stepfather. They found they had no need to fear him, for he always treated them kindly. He was good-natured and loved to tease. One of the first things he did was to build a playhouse next to their smokehouse. Here the girls spent many happy hours in play.

David had a wagon and a fine team of horses. The horses were called Prince and Polly and were well suited to each other. Sam was no longer needed, so they sold him to a neighbor who wanted a good riding pony.

Sometimes in the fall, David would make the long trip to the coast where he would buy salmon from the fishermen. He would buy a large number and would salt them down in a big barrel to take home for the winter. These trips would take nearly a week from the time he left home until he would return again. The roads were rough and muddy, and the wagon mired down in many places, making traveling slow.

Another trip that afforded the entire family a great deal of pleasure was visiting David's own daughter Ida and her family. She and her husband Andrew Erdman had taken up a homestead about eighteen miles northwest of Dallas in a little Valley nestled among the hills. Because of the winding stream through the valley, the creek was called Gooseneck, and the surrounding community was also known by that name.

Andrew and Ida had two little girls, Katie and Annie. They and the Schrag girls enjoyed playing together when Grandpa and Grandma

Unger came to spend the day.

Another smaller stream flowed near Andrew's house, and he had built a springhouse over the running water. Here Ida kept her milk, cream, and butter. The water was cold, and this was an ideal place for her dairy products.

That year marked another turning point in the lives of Barbara and her family. About ten miles north of Eugene in Lane county, an estate of two thousand acres had been put up for sale. This land was mostly cleared, flat, and covered quite thickly with ferns; hence it was known as Fern Ridge. A few oaks and small firs were scattered over the area. When the Mennonites at Dallas heard the property was being sold, a number of them were much interested—so much, in fact, that they immediately made plans to go and look at the land known as the Washburn Estate. They hoped it would prove to be more productive than their hilly farmland had been.

David was among the group making the trip south. Barbara had some misgivings about the advisability of making such a move, but she trusted David's judgment and hoped they would better themselves if David felt it would be a wise undertaking.

The immense tract of land appealed to the men who went to investigate. They decided to purchase the property and form a new settlement. The big estate would be divided among all those who wished to have a share. This group included the Christ Schrags, Jake Schrags, Dan Schrags, Pete Goerings, John Waltners and

David Ungers. They were joined later by several Graber families.

David had forty acres. Before he returned to Dallas for the family, he put up a shed. This building was only partially finished, the whole front side being open.

The Ungers rented their homeplace to Billy Kraber and made plans to move south. They loaded the wagon with household goods and possessions. A hen and eleven baby chicks were imprisoned in a coop at the rear. Barbara and the girls took turns driving the two cows, Blossom and Bloomy, which followed behind the wagon.

The chicks had a hard time surviving, and most of them died on the way. As they were crossing the Luckamute River, Carrie threw the dead chicks one by one into the water.

At night they camped along the road and slept on the ground. It was chilly and uncomfortable, and they were glad when they came to their journey's end. It had taken three days to make the trip.

They moved into the unfinished shed, and Barbara hung blankets over the open end to keep out the cold. Here they would live until they could build a house.

The first night it began to storm. The wind blew hard, and then it began to rain. Outside Prince and Polly sought shelter under a lone fir tree. In the morning when David went out to feed the horses, Polly was missing. Her mate Prince was quietly grazing nearby. David called and searched in vain for the missing horse.

172

At last he discovered some broken boards under the tree. Upon closer examination he was surprised to find an old well. He looked down and to his horror saw Polly. She had backed into the well and been killed by the fall. Only a little bit of water covered the bottom.

The twins were sitting on their blue stools waiting for breakfast when their stepfather came in with the startling news of Polly's tragic death. They all felt bad when they learned of her fate, and the twins sobbed as if their hearts would break.

"There, there. We'll get another horse to take her place," reassured their stepfather kindly. But no one felt much like eating when they gathered around the breakfast table that first morning in their new home.

The horse's death was quite a loss, for David needed to begin hauling lumber for their new home. Fortunately they were soon able to purchase a horse near Irving, and David brought Dolly home. She proved to be a suitable mate for Prince.

David began hauling lumber from the sawmill at Elmira. Soon the house began to take shape as neighbors lent helping hands, and before long they moved into their new home. The lumber was rough and unplaned, but it was a house and much more comfortable than the shed which they had called home those first few months.

Later David put up poles for the framework of a barn. He covered the roof and sides with hand-split shakes.

It was a busy summer in the settlement with all the building going on. The men helped each other, and the women cooked the meals. Then it was time to break the sod so that a beginning could be made on the land. New energy, courage and hope inspired the settlers to try to make good in this newest venture.

Church services were held in their homes, but when the last home was finished, they decided they needed a permanent place of worship. The church building at Dallas was torn down and moved to Fern Ridge where it was rebuilt.

School was also held in the homes, usually at Jake Graber's. The children gathered around the large dining table and at first learned their lessons in German. Later a one-room schoolhouse was built to accommodate the growing number of pupils. By this time they had secured a teacher from town, and the children began to study their lessons in the English language.

That September Fannie and Lillie started their first term of school. Carrie had gone two years at the Liberty School near Dallas.

Annie was now working in Eugene. She was seldom able to come home to visit and missed her family and friends a great deal. But financial conditions at home made it necessary for her to work so that she could contribute her earnings to help provide a living for the family.

# CHAPTER

# 20

It was four years since the wagons had come to Fern Ridge and the colony was founded on the barren tract of land.

Several families belonging to the Old Mennonites had arrived from the eastern states. Among them was young Benjamin Emmert from La Grange, Indiana. Ben was an exceptionally jolly fellow and soon was everyone's friend.

Ben courted and won the heart of Barbara's eldest daughter, and he and Annie were married November 20, 1895, in the little church at Fern Ridge. They set up housekeeping in a small building that had been used as a granary. Annie had worked away from home so long that she could hardly wait to preside as mistress in her own home, and she and Ben were very happy in their humble little dwelling.

Almost a year later their first son, Jesse, was born, and Annie knew the age-old experience of young mothers. This tiny babe in her arms brought a joy that was indescribable.

Carrie, now sixteen, was keeping company with James Mishler, also from Indiana. Jim was quite a few years older than young Carrie. She was vivacious, sparkling, and full of fun, and Jim dearly loved to tease.

There was a growing unrest among the colonists by this time. They had found from the beginning that the soil was poor, and crops were pitifully small for all the hard work. Consequently it was difficult to make a living. Some of the men had been forced to seek employment elsewhere, and this arrangement was anything but satisfactory to these home-loving people.

And so it came about that the entire group felt it best to leave Fern Ridge. The majority made plans to go to the state of Washington. Many of them had relatives in that state, and the country around Ritzville was known as rich wheat farming country. The few remaining families, including the Ungers and Ben Emmerts, would move back to Dallas.

David and Barbara still owned the small acreage they had left, and they moved back into their modest little home. The old familiar surroundings brought back some painful memories to Barbara, but the pain in her heart eased as she threw her whole energy into her efforts to help provide a living for the family. She resumed her work in town, though only occasionally, and these earnings added to their meager income from the farm were their living.

Jim Mishler came to Dallas with the Emmerts, and in August he and dark-eyed Carrie were married. The ceremony took place in the small sitting room at her parents' home. Their first home was a tiny house near Ben's, who lived a few miles away.

The twins returned to school in the fall at Liberty near their home, and life settled back to its daily routine.

Fannie and Lillie loved to visit their married sisters. They usually took the shortcut through the oak grubs and firs up over the hill, since that path was much shorter than the main road. An added attraction was the new baby, Floyd, who had arrived at the home of Annie and Ben.

In the meantime the church building at Fern Ridge was torn down for the second time, brought back to Dallas, and rebuilt— this time at Polk Station about three miles north-east of town.

Three years passed. Lillie and Fannie finished their schooling. They were fifteen and still looked so much alike that their own stepfather had trouble telling them apart.

There were few families left in the little settlement. One by one they had moved away to more desirable locations.

At Hubbard, a new congregation in charge of Jim's father, Bishop J. D. Mishler, was flourishing. Feeling the need of more Christian fellowship and drawn by the climate and fertile soil in that part of the Willamette Valley, three families decided to move to Hubbard.

At this point David astonished the family by saying he thought it best for him to return to his former home in Canada.

"It isn't that I don't love you," he said gently as he discussed this later with Barbara. "You know we have always gotten along well together, but we are both getting older, and I'm not able to earn a living anymore. So I feel it is best for me to live with my children and you with yours."

Barbara consented, though somewhat reluctantly. She didn't want to be a burden to anyone, but if that was the way her husband wanted it, she would be submissive and agree to the arrangement.

Jim and Ben both promised Barbara and the two girls that there would always be a welcome in their homes, and they kept their word. Secretly, however, Jim purposed in his heart as soon as they were settled in their new homes and when David had visited his children, he would insist that "Stepdad," as they affectionately called him, would come back to Oregon and spend his remaining days with them.

So David went to Manitoba, and Barbara and Fannie and Lillie lived alternately with Jim's and Ben's. The girls worked away from home a good share of the time, and Barbara for once in her life began to take things easier. But she soon found that she suddenly seemed to lose her former strength, and her health began to fail. In spite of this, her faith in God remained strong and steadfast, a faith that came from an inner

178

strength built through sorrows and trials.

In the spring Jim and Carrie became the parents of little Raymond. He was a round-faced, chubby baby boy who brought much joy to his parents. Because of some unusual circumstances during his birth, both Jim and Carrie felt that God would have a special work for this child someday. This came true in later years when Raymond was ordained to the ministry, and then to the office of Bishop.

One day Jim approached Fannie while she was in the kitchen making pies. He beckoned to her mysteriously. Fannie wiped the flour from her hands and followed him out to the porch. This brother-in-law of hers was such a tease that she hardly knew what to expect.

But Jim was serious. "I want you to write a letter to Stepdad," he said. "Tell him we want him to come back and live with us. We've got plenty of room and plenty to eat, and as long as we have a crust of bread we'll be glad to share it with him. Will you write the letter and ask him to come?" There was a suspicious moisture in Jim's eyes, and Fannie's heart was touched. It was a noble thing Jim was offering to do.

"Why, yes, Jim, I"ll be more than glad to do it. I'm sure God will reward you for your generosity. I'll write the letter as soon as I get these pies ready for the oven, and you can mail it today. God bless you, Jim." Fannie's voice broke, her emotions deeply stirred. She hurried in to finish her pies.

The letter was written and mailed without

further delay, but the day it reached its destination, friends were digging David's grave. He had passed away very suddenly, and several days after the funeral the news reached Barbara and her family. They all felt very badly, especially Jim, who blamed himself for not having done something sooner. At least their stepfather would have had the pleasure of knowing he was loved and wanted.

About a year after they moved to Hubbard, Bishop George R. Brunk, an eastern evangelist, came west and held a series of meetings at the Hopewell church. This kind of thing was new to the West, and it was during this time of spiritual awakening that Fannie and Lillie accepted Christ as their personal Saviour. On November 16, 1901 they were baptized and received as members into the rapidly growing congregation.

In her early sixties Barbara suffered a light stroke that affected her left arm. Later it was hard for her to get around. However, she spent much of her time piecing quilts for her daughters.

Her grandchildren brought much comfort and joy to Barbara. Since moving to the Hubbard area three more sons, Albert, Ivan, and George, were born to the Emmerts, making a lively family of five boys. Jim and Carrie's family too increased. When Raymond was two, a little girl Florence arrived. Five years later Melvin was born and in another two years, Orval came into their home.

Seated in her rocker with her sewing in her

lap, Barbara was often surrounded by her grandchildren, who begged her to tell them stories of her old home in Russia.

As she reminisced of bygone days, she couldn't help but wonder how she had managed to survive all the hardships she had been called to go through. Even as a little girl in Russia she had suffered to an extent no one would ever know because of circumstances that came into her life at an early age. Then in later years it was only by God's help that she was able to go on.

Barbara sat one day with her hands idly in her lap. The grandchildren had gone off to their play. Her thoughts wandered on. *For His Sake.* The words suddenly flashed into her mind. Where had she heard those words before? Her memory was failing her now, and it was hard to think at times. Ah, yes, it was coming back to her now. Those were the words Grandfather Strauss had used when describing their flight from Germany into Russia so many years ago. Well, it was for His sake too, that they had come to this country so they could enjoy religious freedom. Truly she had much to thank God for in spite of adversities, and she had confidence that she would meet her friends and loved ones before long. Her musings ended as she dozed off into a peaceful little nap.

In 1910 on Thanksgiving Day, Fannie was united in marriage to Daniel Shenk, a fine, Christian young man from Elida, Ohio. The two had met at the conference held at the Hopewell Church. Both young people had been asked to serve as choristers for the day, and they had been asked to occupy the front seat. The situation was a little embarrassing for Fannie, who wondered who the strange young man was. One of the most striking things about him was his luxuriant, dark, curly hair. During the day introductions were made, and the two soon became acquainted. After two years of courtship, they decided to establish a home of their own, and the ceremony was performed at Jim's home in Hubbard.

Lillie was now making her home with the Mishlers. For some time she had been keeping company with Hugh Wolfer, a young man who was working in the butcher shop Jim now owned. Hugh was called "Shortie" by his friends because of his small stature. He had recently become a Christian and was happy in his newfound joy. Worldly pleasures and amusements had lost their attraction for Hugh.

Hugh adored Lillie. In speaking of her to Carrie one day he expressed his true feeling for the girl he loved, ending with these words, "Lillie is an angel on earth." The following summer he and Lillie were married.

Dan and Fannie now had a baby boy whom they named Lloyd. Soon after their marriage they had bought some land about two miles from town. They rented a house, until they were able to clear the land of the trees and stumps, and later build a house and barn. All this took a lot of effort and hard work. Fannie walked out from town every day and carried a lunch for Dan and those who were helping to put up the buildings. They had moved into their new house and were nicely settled when the baby came. A few years later, God laid his hand upon Daniel and he was ordained to be a minister of the Gospel.

By the time Barbara reached her sixty-fifth year her health was very poor, and she had aged rapidly. Her last days were characterized by a slow deterioration, and her once active limbs became almost immobile. She was suffering from diabetes, and her eyesight was almost completely gone, but she bore it patiently and never murmured nor complained.

She was living with Jim's when she became very ill. A bad cold that persisted in hanging on developed into pneumonia, and in spite of all they could do, she departed to be with her Lord on December 9, 1911.

Barbara was laid to rest in the Hopewell Church cemetery near Hubbard, Bishop J. D. Mishler officiating at her funeral.

All who had learned to know and love this courageous, enduring saint would be influenced by the devotion to God and the consistent daily living they had seen her exemplify. They would always remember that for His sake she had suffered, had borne trials patiently, and had overcome.

To the children whom she had reared, this parting meant  thankfulness above grief. As they looked upon the spent, peaceful face of their mother, they thanked God for her release from pain and sorrow. They thanked Him, too, for the wonderful Christian heritage they enjoyed. And along with such a heritage they recognized a challenge for them to accept—a challenge to serve her God more devotedly, to live for His sake as she had done, then to join her at last in eternal rest and peace.

Christian Light Publications, Inc., is a nonprofit conservative Mennonite publishing company providing Christ-centered, Biblical literature in a variety of forms including Gospel tracts, books, Sunday school materials, summer Bible school materials, and a full curriculum for Christian day schools and home schools.

For more information at no obligation or for spiritual help, please write to us at:

Christian Light Publications, Inc.
P. O. Box 1126
Harrisonburg, VA 22801-1126